IMAGES OF WA

THE EASTERN FRONT
AIR WAR
1941–1945

This Soviet wheels-up I-16 fighter, its propeller blades all bent out of shape, gets the once-over by a curious German soldier. It was possible for a pilot to survive such a heavy landing and live to fight another day.

IMAGES OF WAR

THE EASTERN FRONT AIR WAR 1941–1945

RARE PHOTOGRAPHS FROM WARTIME ARCHIVES

Anthony Tucker-Jones

Pen & Sword
MILITARY

First published in Great Britain in 2016 by
PEN & SWORD MILITARY
an imprint of
Pen & Sword Books Ltd,
47 Church Street,
Barnsley,
South Yorkshire
S70 2AS

A CIP record for this book is available from the British Library.

ISBN 978 1 47386 162 6

Typeset by CHIC GRAPHICS

Printed and bound by CPI Group (UK) Ltd, Croydon, CR0 4YY

Pen & Sword Books Ltd incorporates the imprints of Pen & Sword Archaeology,
Atlas, Aviation, Battleground, Discovery, Family History, History, Maritime, Military,
Naval, Politics, Railways, Select, Social History, Transport, True Crime, Claymore
Press, Frontline Books, Leo Cooper, Praetorian Press, Remember When, Seaforth
Publishing and Wharncliffe.

For a complete list of Pen & Sword titles please contact
Pen & Sword Books Limited
47 Church Street, Barnsley, South Yorkshire, S70 2AS, England
E-mail: enquiries@pen-and-sword.co.uk
Website: www.pen-and-sword.co.uk

Contents

Introduction

In the summer of 1941 Stalin's forward defence strategy saw units of the Red Air Force operating from airfields in Soviet-occupied Eastern Poland as well as Western Byelorussia and Ukraine. These included about 7,300 aircraft that were guarding against the threat posed by the Wehrmacht's close proximity in neighbouring Western Poland as well as Hitler's Hungarian and Romanian allies.

Stalin chose to ignore all the warning signs and the ill-prepared Red Air Force paid the price. Air attacks on sixty-six frontier airfields on Sunday, 22 June 1941 heralded Adolf Hitler's titanic assault on Joseph Stalin' Soviet Union, with the result that the Red Air Force was swiftly and efficiently crushed largely still on the ground. The first few days of the war ensured the almost complete destruction of the Red Air Force and left the Red Army at the mercy of the Luftwaffe and Hitler's panzers.

When the time came the Luftwaffe struck – sirens screaming, guns blazing, and bombs whistling from the sky. Some 550 Luftwaffe bombers and 480 fighters were involved in the opening air strikes of Operation Barbarossa. Hitler's strike force also included an additional 300 Stuka dive-bombers from Luftflotten 1, 2 and 4. The dreaded Stuka had made its name as a terror weapon during the Polish campaign in 1939 and, while it enjoyed air superiority, was invincible.

Within the space of five months following Barbarossa the Red Air Force had lost more than 21,000 aircraft in the face of the Luftwaffe's deadly onslaught. Like the Red Army, the Air Force was sent reeling, battered and bleeding. Whilst many of its bombers escaped the opening attacks its fighter force was so severely depleted it seemed at breaking point. Luckily, as many of the fighters were destroyed on the ground, the pilots lived to fight another day. The Soviet Union's cities also felt the wrath of the Luftwaffe; thousands of buildings were shattered into rubble by a steady stream of high explosives delivered by Hitler's Heinkel and Junkers bombers.

The subsequent four-year air war over Russia, or, more precisely, the Soviet Union, is a much neglected aspect of the conflict on the Eastern Front. In particular, it is not generally appreciated that Hitler's strategic blunders in seeking to defeat Stalin were compounded by the inadequacy of his tactical bombers and the needless destruction of his transport fleet. In terms of the conflict in the air the focus of the Second World War has always been on the Battle of Britain, the strategic bomber campaign against Germany, the air campaign supporting the Normandy invasion and the efforts to counter Hitler's V-rockets. The air war on the Eastern Front was no less intense and saw pilots and aircrews on both sides engaged in a deadly duel across vast distances stretching from Leningrad in the far north to the Crimea in the south.

A technological arms race had been taking place throughout the 1930s, which was one that the Soviet Union initially lost. The Soviet aviation design bureaus of MiG, Sukhoi and Yak sought to develop high-speed and agile fighter and interceptor aircraft on a par with those being built in Western Europe. Design flaws and teething problems greatly delayed this process and meant that the bulk of the Soviet Air Force's fighter units were equipped with the obsolete Polikarpov biplanes and monoplanes. These proved incapable of keeping the Luftwaffe at bay.

In addition, in keeping with Stalin's deep mistrust of the Soviet armed forces, he viewed the senior leadership of the air and air defence forces as a serious threat to his power. In consequence they were not spared the purges that afflicted and debilitated the Red Army on the eve of the war. The Red Air Force, in the guise of Stalin's Falcons, and the Luftwaffe, in the shape of Hitler's Condor Legion, gained invaluable combat experience during the Spanish Civil War. Whereas the Luftwaffe's Spanish veterans soon rose through the ranks, Stalin rewarded his Falcons by purging them just before Hitler's invasion. Many of the leading aviation designers and engineers suffered a similar fate. Hampered by poor aircraft, poor training and a dispirited leadership, the Red Air Force proved to be a paper tiger.

In sharp contrast, by the summer of 1941 Hitler's Luftwaffe was riding high thanks to the invaluable experience it had gained supporting the Wehrmacht's hugely successful blitzkrieg in the West. In addition, the Luftwaffe was able to draw on the experience of the German Condor Legion, which had fought for Franco's Nationalists during the Spanish Civil War. Even though the Battle of Britain in the summer of 1940 had provided a wake-up call for the Luftwaffe's deficiencies it was quick to learn from its mistakes, improving its tactics and aircraft.

Thanks to all this, the Messerschmitt Bf 109 developed into a highly proficient fighter and the equally formidable Focke-Wulf Fw 190 was waiting in the wings to join it. Similarly, although Hitler ignored any need for a strategic bomber force, his tactical bombers and dive-bombers gave him a first strike capability that overwhelmed both the Red Air Force and the Red Army in much the same way that he had crushed the French armed forces in May 1940.

In the long term, Hitler's failure to develop a strategic bomber force was to contribute to his downfall on the Eastern Front. Once the Soviets had miraculously evacuated their vital weapon factories east of the Ural Mountains, the Luftwaffe had little means of reaching them. This meant that Hitler was faced with a production war he could not ultimately win. Once the Soviet armed forces began to revitalize and rearm themselves he was faced with a war of attrition that he did not have the resources to fight.

In the West, following Hitler's invasion of the Soviet Union the British and American bomber fleets began to pound his weapons factories with variable accuracy and poor results. Ironically, German output reached an all-time high in 1944. However, the Luftwaffe was increasingly distracted from the fighting on the Eastern Front, first by the Allies' invasion of Italy and Normandy, but mostly because its pilots were forced to fight a defensive war over Germany. The net result was that the Luftwaffe was bled dry on the Eastern Front and was unable to help more than one German Army group at any one time. This in turn impacted on the Luftwaffe's ability to protect its vulnerable air transport fleet, which was conducting ever riskier resupply and casualty evacuation over enormous distances.

Conditions for the pilots and aircrews were appalling in comparison to those in North Africa, the Mediterranean and Western Europe. Fighting on the ground was bad enough, with endless hardship caused by the unforgiving Soviet landscape and the often terrible weather. In the air the danger was greatly magnified and the harsh Russian winter made flying particularly hazardous. The cold added to the hazards endured by both the Luftwaffe and the Red Air Force. Icing caused innumerable accidents both on the ground and in the air. In particular, there was a lack of protective insulation, engines had to be serviced more regularly, hydraulic systems and tyres deteriorated quickly and there was little in the way of special lubricants. During the Battle of Moscow the Red Air Force's pilots were vastly better prepared to cope with the winter conditions than their German counterparts as they had grown up with them.

The Red Air Force was well aware of the dangers posed by the weather, especially after it lost one of its leading test pilots. Highly experienced Valery Chkalov was killed in the winter of 1938 thanks to the engine of his aircraft cutting out as he was coming in to land. Attempting a wheels-up landing, a wing tip brushed the ground and the aircraft cartwheeled. Chkalov was thrown from the cockpit, struck his head and died shortly afterwards. Before take-off he had been warned that the aircraft's engine had not been protected against the frost the previous night, but he decided to gamble with his life and paid the price.

Fortunately for Stalin, the Red Air Force, like the Red Army, not only survived its terrible mauling in 1941–42 but slowly began to recover. Relocated Soviet aviation factories started to churn out ever-growing numbers of fighters, dive-bombers and bombers, while new crews were trained and gained valuable experience.

Whilst the Red Air Force was recovering from the devastating blow from Barbarossa, as well as defending Moscow, Leningrad and Stalingrad the Luftwaffe scored a significant pyrrhic victory at Demyansk. This proved to be the Luftwaffe's undoing on the Eastern Front. In a quite remarkable operation lasting three months, the Luftwaffe maintained an air bridge sustaining 100,000 trapped troops until they were rescued. Convinced that such a heroic feat could be repeated on a grander scale, a year later Hitler ordered the Luftwaffe to supply 250,000 men surrounded in the Russian city of Stalingrad. It was a task too great.

Emboldened by the victory at Stalingrad and a growing confidence the Red Air Force tried to pre-empt Hitler's summer offensive at Kursk. Soviet bombers almost caught the Luftwaffe on its airfields around Kharkov; instead, the Luftwaffe's radar saved them at the eleventh hour and the attacking force, in what was one of the largest air battles of the war, was comprehensively destroyed. This defeat mattered little as the subsequent Battle of Kursk proved to be the Luftwaffe's last major operation on the Eastern Front. The final turning point in the air war over the Soviet Union came in the summer of 1944, when Stalin's massed air fleets supporting the liberation of Byelorussia swept the weakened Luftwaffe before them. From that point on, the Red Air Force harried the Luftwaffe all the way back to Berlin and final victory.

Photograph Sources

All the images in this book are courtesy of the Scott Pick WWII Russian Front Original Photo Collection. This consists of almost 2,500 black and white photographs. They provide a remarkable and often grim insight into the many aspects of the war on the Eastern Front. Notably, the quality of the photographs is consistently high throughout the archive. Most of those selected by the author to illustrate this title have never been published before. Pen & Sword and the author are indebted to Scott Pick for his generous assistance with this project.

Chapter One

Stalin's Falcons Decapitated

Ironically, in the year preceding Hitler's invasion, as the Red Air Force's numerical strength grew its effectiveness declined. This was in part due to its loss of technical parity with other European air forces, as well as the setbacks it experienced in Spain during the Spanish Civil War and in the Winter War with Finland. The Red Air Force was slow to learn from these hard-won lessons and in common with the Red Army suffered thanks to the destruction of its high command by Stalin.

The Red Air Force was not immune to Stalin's purges during the late 1930s. General Ya. I. Alksnis, Red Air Force Commander-in-Chief, and General A.I. Sedyakin, Air Defence Commander-in-Chief, were shot during the Soviet leader's paranoid bloodletting. The execution of the former Red Air Force commander, General Ya. V. Smushkevich, occurred four months after the German invasion, Smushkevich having been dismissed in 1940. His replacement, Pavel Rychagov, lost his job in the spring of 1941 to Pavel Zhigarev. According to German intelligence the actual strength of the air force prior to the invasion was about 30 per cent less than the authorized establishment. Stalin's air force, like the rest of the Soviet armed forces, was not in the best condition to fend off Hitler's blitzkrieg.

Stalin, who was almost the architect of his own destruction, did all he could to derail the modernization of the Red Air Force. Alksnis' crime was being too closely associated with the discredited modernizer Marshal Tukhachevsky. He was on his way to a diplomatic reception in Moscow when, on 23 November 1937, he was grabbed and whisked away to the Lubyanka prison: he was dead in less than year.

Alksnis was not alone; most of his comrades suffered the same fate, including Chief of the Air Staff and Head of the Special Purpose Air Arm Vasily Khripin, Head of the Air Force Political Directorate B.U. Troyanker, and Head of the Zhukovsky Air Force Academy General A.I. Todorski, along with five military district air commanders. Only a year before, these men had received decorations from Stalin himself.

Alksnis' initial replacement did not prove up to the job and was replaced by the highly experienced Smushkevich ready for the invasion of Eastern Poland in 1939. Under the nom de guerre General Douglas, Brigade Commander Yakov Vladimirovich Smushkevich commanded the Soviet Air Group in Spain known as

Stalin's Falcons. They combat tested the Soviet Union's I-15 and I-16 fighters as well as the SB-2 bomber. Smushkevich then went on to command the Red Air Force, supporting General Georgy Zhukov's brief and highly successful border war against the Japanese on the Mongolian–Manchurian border. Smushkevich was unable to repeat his Manchurian successes over Finland and the poor condition of the Red Air Force was highlighted during the Winter War, which broke out in November 1939 and was fought through three and a half months of freezing weather.

Smushkevich had 900 aircraft available for operations against less than 100 Finnish planes. Nonetheless, they suffered heavy losses, especially the obsolescent SB, DB-3 and TB-3 bombers. Large-scale Soviet bombing raids failed to achieve much and ground support was poorly coordinated. By the time the war with the Finns came to an end the Red Air Force had massed 2,000 aircraft against Finland. Despite much backslapping the Soviets lost up to 950 aircraft whilst the Finns lost just seventy. It was a hard-won victory that showed the Red Air Force to be a largely flawed instrument.

In April 1940 Smushkevich was sacked and replaced by his former brother-in-arms Pavel Rychagov. He was another of Stalin's Falcons, credited with fifteen victories in Spain and named as a Hero of the Soviet Union. Rychagov also saw action against the Japanese in Manchuria. Commissioned as a fighter pilot in Ukraine, he rose in four short years from squadron leader to head of the Red Air Force, only to be swept away in Stalin's purges barely two months before Hitler's invasion. He lasted until the spring of 1941, to be replaced by Pavel Zhigarev (another commander from the Soviet Far East) in what must have felt like an unending game of deadly musical chairs. Smushkevich was shot on 28 October 1941, depriving the Red Air Force of his valuable expertise.

The Soviet aircraft industry suffered as well; A.N. Tupolev, head of the Experimental Aircraft Design Section, was arrested on the ludicrous charge of having sold the plans for the Bf 109 and Bf 110 fighters to Germany! His senior design team, including Vladimir Petlyakov and Vladimir Myasishchev, soon joined him. An estimated 450 designers and engineers were interned from 1934 to 1941. Of these, fifty were executed and 100 died in the Gulag.

At the same time, many of the aircraft factories lost key personnel, including directors, chief engineers and designers. The failures of prototypes to meet performance criteria and accidents during test flights were considered deliberate sabotage. When Valery Chkalov was killed in the prototype I-180 fighter on 15 December 1938, the death of this national hero led to a wave of arrests despite the accident being down to pilot error. This fighter was abandoned shortly afterwards, depriving the Red Air Force of 3,000 I-180s that would have been in service by June 1941.

The Soviet armed forces were divided into five elements prior to the Second World War: the ground forces, navy, air force, national air defence and armed forces support. The ground forces accounted for the largest proportion of personnel, with just over 79 per cent. The Red Air Force had just over 11 per cent and the navy had just under 6 per cent. The Red Air Force consisted of four key elements: the Voenno-Vozdushnye Sily (VVS – Air Force), Protivovozdushnaya Oborona (PVO – Air Defence), the Fleet Air Force and Gosudarstvenny Komitet Oborony (GKO – State Committee for Defence) Air Reserve.

The Soviet Union claimed to have the world's largest air force in 1940, but in reality 75 per cent of them were obsolete I-15, I-152 and I-153 biplanes and I-16 monoplanes. Whilst the I-16 was the best, it was significantly inferior to the German Bf 109E. Their new LaGG-3, MiG-3 and Yak-1 had yet to be issued in any number although by 22 June 1941, about 2,030 of these aircraft had been produced.

Initially, a Soviet fighter regiment consisted of three squadrons with an established strength of forty aircraft. These squadrons flew tight defensive formations with three or four aircraft known as Zveno. A fighter aviation division was made up of three regiments, with a nominal strength of 120 aircraft. These divisions were grouped in two or threes to create aviation army corps with strength of up to 375 fighters.

At the outbreak of the war the mainstay of the Red Air Force's fighter squadrons were aircraft designed by Nikolai N. Polikarpov. The Polikarpov I-16 was first flown in late December 1933 and was the first production monoplane in the world to feature a retractable undercarriage. It was also the first Soviet fighter to incorporate armour plating around the cockpit. Introduced into service in 1934, this aircraft had a number of major design faults; most notably, the engine was too close to the centre of gravity and the cockpit was too far back. This gave the airframe insufficient longitudinal stability, making it impossible to fly 'hands off'.

Taking off and landing was not pilot friendly, either. The pilot had to hand crank the undercarriage forty-four times before retraction was complete. When deployed the undercarriage suspension was hard, which meant the aircraft had a habit of bouncing violently when it ran over uneven ground. This gained it the nickname *Ishak* (donkey). Nonetheless, in the hands of an experienced pilot the I-16 proved to be highly manoeuvrable. The I-16 saw combat in Spain with Stalin's Falcons against the Spanish Republicans and against the Japanese in the Far East. The Spanish Nationalist Air Force christened it the *Rata* (rat). This nickname stuck and was used by the Luftwaffe.

Despite its shortcomings, by the time production ceased in 1940 some 6,555 I-16s had been built. Variants included the TsKB-18 assault aircraft armed with four PV-1 synchronized machine guns, two wing-mounted machine guns and 100kg of bombs. The Type 17 featured two wing-mounted cannon and this variant was built in large numbers. The TskB-12P was the first aircraft in the world to be armed with two synchronized cannon firing through the propeller arc. The last fighter version the Type 24 was capable of a top speed of 523km/h (325mph).

The Polikarpov I-153 was first flown in 1938 and was derived from the I-15 biplane fighter. The latter had featured a gull-type upper wing, while the following variant, the I-15bis (or I-152) was fitted with a straight wing. The I-153 reverted to the gull wing arrangement, resulting in it being dubbed the *Chaika* (seagull). Unlike its predecessor it featured a retractable undercarriage. A series of engine upgrades eventually gave the *Chaika* a top speed of 426km/h (265mp).

The pilot sat in an open cockpit with only a small windscreen for protection. The aircraft was armed with four synchronized machine guns firing along canals between the engine cylinders. A few were also fitted with two 20mm cannon. The *Chaika* first saw action in 1939 against the Japanese. It was also heavily involved in the Winter War of 1939–40, when the Soviet Union clashed with Finland. The I-153 was simply too slow against the Luftwaffe and was the last single-seat fighter biplane built in the Soviet Union.

The Soviets were late in developing an effective monoplane in the same class as the British Hurricane and Spitfire and the German Bf 109. The Yak fighter sought to address this shortcoming. The Yak-1 *Krasavyets* (beauty) first appeared publicly on 7 November 1940. This was Aleksandr S. Yakovlev's very first fighter design, powered by a 746kW (1,000hp) M-105PA engine armed with a nose-mounted 20mm cannon and two machine guns. This was a crude aircraft; there were no flying blind instruments and no fuel gauges! The gunsight was rudimentary, as was the cockpit equipment. Visibility was poor thanks to the four-piece cockpit canopy. Capable of 600km/h (373mph), it was reportedly a pleasure to fly and easy to maintain. Unfortunately, the German invasion disrupted production while the aviation factories were evacuated.

As a wartime expedient it was decided to convert the two-seat trainer variant, the Yak-7V, into a single-seat fighter by covering the second cockpit. This aircraft was redesignated the Yak-7A, but during 1942 the basic Yak-1 evolved into the slightly improved Yak-1M with a three-piece sliding hood, revised rear fuselage and smaller wing area. Likewise, the Yak-7A was upgraded to the Yak-7B, of which 6,399 were produced. Refinements to the Yak-1M before the aircraft entered quantity production in early 1943 led to the Yak-3. Some of these were heavily armed; for example, the Yak-3K was equipped with a 45mm cannon and the Yak-3T with a 37mm cannon. Another variant, the Yak-9, which was a further development of the Yak-7, entered service in 1942 and became the most mass-produced Soviet fighter.

In late 1939, the design bureau of Artem I. Mikoyan and Mikhail I. Guryevich was ordered to come up with a single-seat, single-engine monoplane interceptor. Within four months they had produced a prototype, which went into production as the MiG-1. Whilst the aircraft had a high performance, this came at a price, with armament being sacrificed in favour of a heavy, high-altitude engine that gave it a speed of 640km/h (398mph).

The MiG-1 was handicapped by the length of its engine, which resulted in poor pitch and directional stability. In addition, following Russian tradition the pilot had to endure high altitudes and high speed in an open cockpit. Despite being difficult to fly and unstable it was rushed into production. The weight of the engine meant that it could only carry one nose-mounted 12.7mm machine gun and two 7.62mm machine guns in the wings. After the first 100 MiG-1s had been built the aircraft was improved and redesignated the MiG-3. This featured a fully enclosed cockpit and an auxiliary fuel tank. Its increased range led to the MiG-3 being employed for fighter reconnaissance roles.

The MiG was needed as a matter of urgency to arm the fighter regiments of the Air Defence Force (PVO) created in early 1941 and by the end of June 1941, 1,309 MiGs had been produced compared to 399 Yak-1 and 322 LaGG fighters. The MiG-3 was the most prolific of the three new types of fighter at the outbreak of war. From equipping just 10 per cent of the front-line force in mid-1941, this rose to 41 per cent by the end of the year.

The MiG-3's ability at high altitude made it a good tactical reconnaissance aircraft, but at low to medium altitude it was no match for the Bf 109E/F. During the Battle of Moscow the MiG-3 was also used as a night fighter. Despite attempts to improve them, MiG fighters were never a match for the Lavochkin or Yakovlev designs.

The LaGG-3 was one of the most modern fighter aircraft available to the Red Air Force at the time of the German invasion, having just come into service in early 1941. Designed by Semyon A. Lavochkin, the LaGG-3, although well armed with a 20mm cannon and two machine guns, proved to be heavy – slower than the MiG or Yak and hard to control. As a result it was very unpopular with pilots. Whilst the LaGG-3 had similar armament to the Bf 109, crucially it was slower, heavier and much less manoeuvrable. Some 6,528 LaGG-3s had been produced by 1944, before production in Tbilisi had been switched to the Yak-3.

The vastly improved Lavochkin LaGG-3 – known as the La-5 – did not enter service until July 1942 and was followed by the La-7 in 1944. These acted as low- and medium-level fighters. They were also sometimes used in a ground-attack role. Production of the La-5/La-7 series amounted to 21,975 aircraft by the end of the war.

Confident looking Red Air Force pilots photographed in 1939 during the fighting in Mongolia against the Japanese. Stalin's Falcons gained valuable combat experience fighting in Spain, Finland and Mongolia during the late 1930s. Behind them is a Polikarpov I-16 fighter.

The Polikarpov I-16 was initially flown on 31 December 1933. It was the first production monoplane to have a retractable undercarriage and was the first Soviet fighter to have armoured plating protecting the pilot. At the time of the German invasion it provided the mainstay of the Red Air Forces' fighter squadrons. Both these aircraft appear to have suffered violent crash-landings before falling into German hands. It is also conceivable that the second aircraft was caught on the ground by the Luftwaffe's opening assault on the Soviet Union, although the dent to the lower part of the engine cover indicates it made a nose-down landing.

Two views of the two-seat training version of the I-16, known as the UTI (there were three models, known as the UTI-1, UTI-2 and UTI-4, based on the Type 1 and Type 5 I-16). These are the UTI-4, which featured fixed landing gear, making them slightly easier to handle. About 3,400 of these were produced; they became scrap after the German invasion.

The Polikarpov I-153 biplane fighter was first flown in 1938 and features a very distinctive gull-shaped upper wing; this gained it the nickname *Chaika* (seagull). This wing also featured on the I-15, but unlike its predecessor the I-153 had retractable landing gear. This aircraft seems to have been shot up on the ground and never got airborne to meet its attackers.

The *Chaika* first saw combat against the Japanese over Mongolia during the Battle of Khalkhin Gol in 1939. This aircraft came off worse against the Japanese Air Force.

Rows of captured I-153 in various states of repair. The Germans made no effort to reuse captured Soviet aircraft after they had overrun the Red Air Force's air bases.

The Yakolev Yak-1 *Krasavyets* (beauty) was an attempt to produce a fighter on par with the British Hurricane and the German Bf109. However, the four-piece cockpit canopy resulted in poor visibility, and the instrumentation and gunsight were primitive. It appeared in 1940 and led to the more successful Yak-1M and Yak-7A.

SOV. YAK.1

A German cyclist stops to watch a souvenir hunter searching a Yak-1 fighter, which seems to have made a remarkable crash-landing in a dry riverbed and survived the impact.

A Soviet wartime expedient was the Yak-7A fighter, which was a conversion of the Yak-7V trainer.

The remains of a wheels-up crash-landed Yak-1. This aircraft was of mixed construction; fabric and plywood covered the aluminium airframe. In total, 8,721 of these aircraft were produced.

The smashed remains of MiG-3 fighters that had only just come into service in 1941. At low to medium altitude it proved no match for the Luftwaffe's Bf 109. As both aircraft are resting on their undercarriage it is likely that they were amongst the thousands of Red Air Force fighters destroyed on the ground by the Luftwaffe in the first few hours of Hitler's Operation Barbarossa.

Chapter Two

The Falcon's Shturmoviks

The Red Air Force was equipped with a number of rickety biplanes that looked like relics from the First World War, which acted as Shturmoviks, or ground-attack aircraft. Key amongst these was the robust Polikarpov two-seat U-2 trainer (renamed the Po-2 in 1944). It was nicknamed *Kukuruznik* (crop duster) and despite its rather ancient appearance proved highly successful in both civilian and military service. Designed by Nikolai Polikarpov, it was intended as a replacement for the earlier U-1 Avrushka trainer aircraft.

The U-2 was used widely on the Eastern Front in a variety of roles including ground attack, night bomber, air ambulance, supply plane and staff liaison. It was first used as a bomber in 1941, and was deployed as a light bomber and for reconnaissance during the defence of Odessa. Although its slow speed meant much faster enemy fighters found it hard to shoot at, it was vulnerable to anti-aircraft fire. Therefore the following year it was redeployed as a light, night ground-attack aircraft. In the darkness the sound of the engine reminded German troops of a sewing machine and they dubbed it the *Nähmaschine*. Its main claim to fame was with the Night Witches – an all-women night bomber regiment. The fact that about 20,000 U-2s were built by the end of the war is testament to the aircraft's utility.

Two other biplanes in service were the two-seat R-5 and R-Z, which were also reconnaissance and light bomber aircraft. The former went into production in 1930 and 5,000 were built for the Red Air Force. The R-5 was flown by the Spanish Republican Air Force during the Spanish Civil War. It was deployed by the Soviets and the Mongolian People's Air Force against the Japanese during the Battle of Khalkhin Gol in 1939; it then supported the Soviet invasion of Poland and saw action against the Finns in the Winter War. The R-5Sh was a ground-attack variant armed with four wing-mounted machine guns. Various versions of the R-5 were employed by the Soviets until 1944.

The R-Z, introduced in 1935, was a development of the improved R-5SSS and included a sliding canopy for the crew. The production run was short-lived and by the time it came to a close in the spring of 1937, only just over a thousand R-Zs had been built. Like the R-5 it also saw combat with the Spanish Republican Air Force and against the Japanese and the Finns. By the time of the German invasion it was being phased out by the Il-2, but still remained with a few light bomber regiments. Limited numbers of the Yakolev UT-1 monoplane single-seat trainer were used for reconnaissance work and ground attack in the opening stages of the war. Ground-attack conversions known as the UT-1B saw action over Sevastopol and the Caucasus in 1942.

Pavel Sukhoi's initial contribution to the Red Air Force was the ill-fated single-engine Su-2 short-range light bomber, which bears a passing resemblance to Japanese dive-bombers. It was to prove nowhere near as effective. In the mid-1930s, Stalin had issued a requirement for a multipurpose combat aircraft that could both scout and attack targets at the same time. Sukhoi, who was with the Tupolev aviation design bureau, worked on this project, which was dubbed 'Ivanov'.

It went into production as the two-seat BB-1 (Blizhniy Bombardirovschik, or short-range bomber) but in 1940 was renamed the Su-2 following the convention of using the first two letters of the designer's surname. Work also commenced on a ground-attack version known as the ShB but this was dropped in favour of the Il-2. Similarly, an upgraded and more heavily armed version called the Su-4 only got as far as the prototype stage.

The Su-2 was just going into mass production when the war broke out and the factory at Kharkov had to be relocated, disrupting the process. At the beginning of the war the factory was producing three aircraft per day. By September 1941, this had risen to five and it was intended to equip seven regiments. During the early stages of the war the Su-2 bombers were used in combat. Although the aircraft's armament was considered insufficient it successfully flew short-range bombing, reconnaissance and artillery spotting operations. The Su-2 took part in the fighting near Lvov, Kiev, Moscow and Stalingrad as well as the battles for Orel and Kursk.

On 12 September 1941, after she was attacked by seven Bf 109s and ran out of ammunition, female pilot Yekaterina Zelenko, flying her burning Su-2 near the town of Sumy, fatally rammed a Bf 109. It was the first and only ramming attack by a woman pilot in the history of air combat. Like the British Fairey Battle light bomber, the Su-2 proved highly vulnerable to enemy fighters and 222 were destroyed during the German invasion. Production ceased in 1942, by which time only 889 had been built and the remaining operational Su-2s were replaced by the more reliable Il-2, Pe-2 and Tu-2 bombers.

The Red Air Force had two new ground-attack aircraft – the Il-2 and the Pe-2. The single-seat Ilyushin Il-2 Shturmovik completed its acceptance trials in March 1941 and 249 had been built just before the German invasion in June. The initial model lacked a rear-gun position and suffered heavy loses in its early career against the Luftwaffe's fighters. Various upgrades were made to the single-seat variant but it was not until August 1943 that the much more successful two-seat was produced. This was the Il-2m3, armed with cannon, machine guns, bombs and rockets and capable of 404km/h (251mph). It was to play a decisive role, especially in the Battle of Kursk, where Shturmoviks mauled the 2nd and 3rd Panzer divisions. By the end of the war a total of 36,183 Il-2 Shturmoviks had been built, more than any other aircraft in history.

Similarly, the twin-engine Petlyakov Pe-2 dive-bomber only went into production in February 1941, with just over 460 delivered by the time of the German invasion. This aircraft could manage 580km/h (360mph) and was armed with six machine guns, along with 1,600kg of bombs. It took a crew of three, with the pilot and navigator/bombardier in tandem. The third crew member acted as the radio operator/rear gunner and was installed in a separate rear compartment that was accessed by a hatch in the upper fuselage. The ventral machine gun was aimed by the radio operator with the aid of a periscope.

A lack of trained aircrews greatly hampered the aircraft's deployment and only a few saw action during the opening stages of the fighting. The Pe-2 was not committed in any numbers until August 1941, when they were used to make low-level attacks on German columns. By the second half of 1941, a further 1,405 aircraft had been delivered. The Pe-2 proved to be an excellent tactical dive-bomber and was comparable to the British Mosquito. By war's end, total production of the Pe-2/3 amounted to 11,425 aircraft.

The Soviets' light bomber fleet largely comprised the twin-engine SB-2, designed by Andrei N. Tupolev in the early 1930s. It went into production in 1936, and 6,967 had been built before production ended in 1941. Although it saw action during the Spanish Civil War and in the Winter War, by the time of the German invasion it was obsolescent. In Spain it was considered invulnerable because it was faster than most fighters in service at that time. However, the SB-2 suffered losses when making daylight attacks against the Germans so was switched to night bombing. The vastly superior twin-engine Tupolev Tu-2 did not enter service until the spring of 1944 and although only 1,111 were built it played a key part in the Red Army's final offensives towards Berlin.

Like the Germans and the Italians, the Soviets paid little heed to developing strategic bombers, instead concentrating on tactical support. The four-engine Petlyakov Pe-8 was the only Soviet Strategic bomber to see service during the war. Work commenced in the mid-1930s and it entered service in 1940. In the summer of 1941 it carried out the little-known first strategic attack of the war when a small force reached Berlin. Development of the Pe-8 was greatly hampered by inadequate engines and by 1944 only seventy-nine had been built. Some did play a limited role in attacking German armour concentrations during the Battle of Kursk.

German officers inspect a captured Soviet Yakolev U-1 trainer, while to the right is an I-16. The Polikarpov two-seat U-2 *Kukuruznik* (crop duster) was designed to replace the U-1.

This German soldier is sitting on a U-2 or R-5 light reconnaissance bomber. Up to 20,000 U-2s were built for the Red Air Force and the aircraft saw combat throughout the war in a variety of guises.

The Soviet R-5 first went into service in 1930 and by the time it had been phased out fourteen years later, about 7,000 had been built.

The BB-1 *Blizhniy Bombardirovschik*, or short-range bomber, was renamed the Su-2 in 1940. Production was disrupted by the German invasion and the aircraft proved to be vulnerable to enemy fighters.

Two views of the initial single-seat Il-2 Shturmovik, or ground-attack, aircraft, which was armed with 20mm or 23mm cannon depending on which factory produced it. Due to the shortage of fighters in 1941–42, the Il-2 was sometimes used as a fighter, but it was outclassed by the Bf 109 and the Fw 190 with predictable results. However, the Il-2's firepower proved quite effective against the German Hs 126, Ju-87 and Ju-52.

The Il-2M with a rear gunner entered service in September 1942 and the remaining single-seat versions were converted to this configuration. The Il-2m3 with the NS-37 37mm cannon seen here appeared the following year featuring swept-back arrow wings. The Red Army called it the 'Hunchback' and the 'Flying Tank' and it proved deadly against German armour.

The Petlyakov Pe-2 dive-bomber, nicknamed *Peshka* (pawn, i.e. 'little Pe') went into production in February 1941. The version pictured here is the Pe-3, which was a night fighter variant. The Pe-2 proved to be a highly capable aircraft that could escape the Luftwaffe's interceptors and was able to take on the Bf 109.

The burnt remains of a Pe-2 shot from the skies by the Luftwaffe. German pilots soon discovered the aircraft's weakness lay with the ventral gun, which had limited angles of fire and tended to jam. Also, the rear gunner was poorly protected, leaving him vulnerable to enemy fire.

The Tupolev SB twin-engine light bomber went into production in the mid-1930s, and 6,967 had been built by 1941. It proved vulnerable making daylight raids so was switched to night bombing.

The Pe-8 was the only four-engine Soviet strategic bomber to see service during the war but a mere seventy-nine were ever built. Just before Operation Barbarossa only the 2nd Squadron, 14th Heavy Bomber Regiment was equipped with the Pe-8 and it was not combat ready.

The TB-3 bomber, introduced in 1932 having seen action over Mongolia and Finland, was officially withdrawn from service in 1939. Nonetheless, the Red Air Force had 516 and the navy another twenty-five aircraft, and by the summer of 1941 it made up 25 per cent of the Soviet bomber force.

This captured Soviet airfield contains a wide variety of aircraft types, which, left to right, includes SB-2 light bombers, Su-2 short-range bombers, an I-15 trainer and a U-2 reconnaissance aircraft.

The smashed remains of an Ilyuhsin, or Tupolev, twin-engine bomber.

Chapter Three

Hitler's Eagles

Under Reichsmarschall Hermann Göring, in his role as air minister and commander of the Luftwaffe, Hitler's air force grew rapidly. It was considered the branch of the Wehrmacht that had the closest bonds to the Nazi Party, and attracted eager recruits. Göring built a force of 400,000 personnel and 4,000 aircraft, which played a key role in the success of Hitler's blitzkrieg both in the West and the Balkans during 1940–41.

According to German sources the Luftwaffe had just under 2,000 aircraft available for Operation Barbarossa – supporting Army Group North in Luftflotte 1 under Keller, supporting Army Group Centre in Luftflotte 2 under Kesselring and supporting Army Group South with Luftflotte 4 under Löhr. However, only 1,300 of these were serviceable on the day of the invasion. In contrast, Soviet intelligence, including the Romanian Air Force and Luftflotte 5 in Finland and Norway, put the Luftwaffe strength at 3,500.

Soviet air strength was never officially confirmed, but 1,540 of the newer aircraft representing 20 per cent of Soviet air power in the Western Soviet Union were available when Hitler invaded. Including the older airframes, it was assessed there were at least 7,300 Soviet aircraft in the west of the country. An additional 3,500 to 4,000 aircraft were in service in the central Soviet Union and the Soviet Far East representing a vast reserve, although most were obsolescent types.

Hitler was gambling that superior technology and tactics would give him the edge he needed to overcome the Red Air Force and the Red Army. Whatever the Soviets' true air strength in the western military districts it is evident that it outnumbered the Luftwaffe by some considerable margin in the region of 7:1.

Undoubtedly the Luftwaffe's jewel in the crown in 1941 was the Messerschmitt Bf 109 fighter. It provided the mainstay of the Luftwaffe's fighter squadrons for most of the war and was at the forefront of Barbarossa. The prototype flew in the summer of 1935 and the first production model was the Bf 109B, powered by a 455kW (610hp) Jumo 210 engine. When the Second World War broke out the Luftwaffe's fighter units had more than a thousand of these aircraft, which included Bf 109C and Bf 109D, which were in the process of being replaced by the newer E series. The latter provided the backbone of the fighter squadrons throughout 1940. During the Battle of Britain the Bf 109 was used as an escort fighter, a role for which it was not intended; it was also used for photo reconnaissance and as a fighter-bomber.

The Bf 109E-4 differed from the more numerous E-3 in having an improved cannon with an increased rate of fire; otherwise the armament was identical. The two 20mm cannon were mounted in the wings and a pair of 7.92mm machine guns were mounted in the upper forward fuselage. The E-4 was capable of 575km/h (357mph) with a range of 660km (410 miles). The Bf 109F came into service in May 1941 and was superior in many aspects to the RAF's Hurricane and Spitfire. It was to prove a very effective fighter during the invasion of the Soviet Union. This aircraft differed from its predecessor, having a cleaner airframe, redesigned wing rail assembly, radiators and engine cowling. In late 1942, yet another variant appeared, designated the Bf 109G.

Overall, Bf 109 production amounted to about 35,000 aircraft and played a key part in all the air battles of the Second World War. One of the main drawbacks with this successful fighter was that the unstable narrow-track undercarriage, which retracted outwards into the wings, often caused landing accidents. On the rough terrain of Byelorussia and Ukraine pilots had to be careful taking off or landing on rough airstrips.

The Focke-Wulf Fw 190 fighter did not go into service until after the invasion of the Soviet Union. It first appeared as an interim fighter designed to complement the Bf 109, and the first production model, the Fw 190A-1, was deployed on occupation duties to France in the summer of 1941. Early production Fw 190s were armed with four machine guns mounted in the upper fuselage and wing roots. This proved inadequate firepower and aircraft were retrofitted with heavier cannon in each outer wing. The Fw 190 became known as the Butcher Bird by its opponents, which says much for its killing power over other fighters. When it made its appearance in the autumn of 1941 it established Luftwaffe superiority for some months. The following year it began to replace the Bf 109 in Western Europe but the latter continued to serve in a variety of roles on the Eastern Front.

Improvements led to the Fw 190A-2, which had a longer span and heavier armament. This, in turn, was followed by the excellent A-3 fighter-bomber. These were supplemented by the A-4 and A-5, with some of the latter modified as two-seat trainers. The Fw 190A-6 featured a lighter wing and armament of four 20mm cannon. The A-7 appeared in late 1943, equipped with two cannon and two machine guns. The final A-8 had two machine guns and could carry up to four cannon, plus bombs and rockets. More than 20,000 of all types of Fw 190s were produced. The wide-track undercarriage of the Fw 190 meant that it was much more forgiving in the hands of an inexperienced pilot than the Bf 109. Also, as a result, it was much better than the Bf 109 operating from rough airfields so made it ideal for the Eastern Front. However, there were never enough available. Most were kept back to defend the skies over the Reich.

The twin-engine Messerschmitt Bf 110D-1 came into being in the 1930s as a long-range escort fighter but suffered heavy losses as a day fighter in the Battle of Britain. Although it was fast and heavily armed it was no match for the Hurricane and Spitfire. The Bf 110 was armed with four 7.92mm machine guns staggered in the upper nose and two 20mm cannon mounted in the lower fuselage beneath the pilot's seat. The aircraft was intended to carry three crew (pilot, radio operator and gunner); in practice, just two were carried, with the radio operator doubling up as the gunner.

It soon evolved into a ground-attack aircraft. The D-2 was employed in both fighter and bomber modes, whilst the D-3 was the D-1 with bomb racks. The Bf 110E-1 and E-2 carried bombs under their wings in addition to larger bombs under the fuselage. Whilst the Bf 110 proved a failure as a long-range escort fighter it came into its own as the G-4 night fighter.

The Luftwaffe's key dive-bombers, or Sturzkampfflugzeug, were the Henschel Hs 123 and the more famous Junkers Ju 87 Stuka. The latter, with its wailing dive siren, came to epitomise the terror of Hitler's unstoppable blitzkrieg. The biplane prototype of the former first flew in May 1935, but the programme did not get off to a good start after two prototypes lost their wings during test dives. The first five Hs 123As were sent to Spain in 1936 for evaluation with the Condor Legion. The resulting Hs 123B was given a ground-attack role rather than dive-bombing. These went on to see combat during the German invasions of Poland, France and the Soviet Union.

Although the Hs 123 was only lightly armed with two machine guns and up to 450kg of bombs, the loud engine proved an ideal weapon for spreading panic amongst the enemy. The Hs 123C variant was armed with a more powerful 20mm cannon. The aircraft's open cockpit made it a rather grim aircraft to operate on the Eastern Front during the winter although the heat from the radial engine partly compensated for this. The Henschel Hs 123 was the Luftwaffe's last operational biplane and remained in action in the East until 1944.

The first prototype Ju 87V-1 flew in the late spring of 1935; the finalized design went into production two years later. The Ju 87B and extensively modified version appeared in 1938, employing the more powerful 820kW (1,100hp) Jumo 211Da engine. The next production model was the Ju 87D, of which there were a number of variants. It had a speed of 410km/h (255mph) and a range of 1,535km (954 miles). The last model was the Ju 87G, a standard Ju 87D-5 converted to carry two BK 37 cannon under the wings.

The Stuka's highly distinctive inverted gull wing had pylons for two 250kg or four 50kg bombs. The bomb cradle ensured that the bombs, once released in a dive, would swing clear of the propeller. The shape of the wings also allowed the fixed undercarriage to be kept short, which reduced drag. The pilot and rear gunner sat under a sliding canopy protected by substantial armour. The aircraft included an automatic dive control feature that could pull the Ju 87 out of a dive at a preset altitude. During the Battle of Britain the Stuka was found to be vulnerable without local air superiority. After heavy losses at the hands of the RAF it was withdrawn from the fight over the British Isles.

The Luftwaffe's bomber force comprised the Dornier Do 17, Heinkel He 111 and Junkers Ju 88. The Dornier was capable of carrying 1,000kg (2,205lb) of bombs and in the early part of the war was used in bomber and reconnaissance roles. The major production version was the Dornier Do17Z, and a total of 1,700 were built from 1939 to 1940. Although the Do 17 was deployed in the invasion of the Soviet Union, most had been withdrawn from front-line service by late 1941. The Do 217, although looking like an enlarged Do 17, was essentially an entirely new aircraft that started life as a reconnaissance aircraft and then progressed to bomber and night-fighter roles.

The He 111B was combat tested with the Condor Legion in Spain in 1937. Two years later, the 111P appeared, but this was switched to the 111H – the variant that formed the backbone of the Luftwaffe's bomber force from 1940 to 1943. This could deliver 4,000kg (8,818lb) of bombs. By 1944, when production came to an end, about 6,150 had been built.

The Ju 88A was first delivered to the Luftwaffe in 1939 and it proved to be one of the most versatile German aircraft of the war, serving in a wide variety of roles. It saw considerable action in the Balkans, the Mediterranean and on the Eastern Front. The Ju 88A was fitted with four under-wing racks, each of which could carry 500kg (1,100lb) of bombs. The fuselage bays could take up to twenty-eight 50kg (110lb) bombs. By the end of 1942, the Luftwaffe had taken receipt of more than 8,000 Ju 88s, with total production amounting to almost 15,000 aircraft.

In the year before Hitler's attack on the Soviet Union the Luftwaffe's high-altitude reconnaissance units were kept busy mapping Soviet airfields in Eastern Poland and Byelorussia. Stalin chose to ignore these intrusions for fear of provoking Hitler. Soviet pilots desperately wanted to see off these flagrant violations of their air space but were told to stand down. By 1941, the Luftwaffe's aerial spies had identified half of the Red Air Force's 200 operational airfields between Murmansk in the north and Rostov-on-Don in the far south. In total, it had in excess of a thousand airfields but the rest were dormant. Stalin's doctrine of forward defence meant that the Red Air Force was based in Soviet-occupied Eastern Poland and could be easily reached from the German-occupied zone, so intelligence gathering in this region was extensive.

Luftwaffe intelligence assessed that the Red Air Force and supporting bombers of the long-range aviation units had some 7,300 aircraft deployed in the Western Soviet Union. This, though, did not take into account the 1,500 aircraft of the Soviet Navy (supporting the Artic, Baltic and Black Sea fleets) and the 1,445 aircraft of the PVO air defence regiments. In total, the Red Air Force actually had up to 14,000 aircraft available in the Western Soviet Union. In the key five border military districts (Leningrad, Baltic, Western, Kiev and Odessa) these numbered some 5,440 aircraft, including 2,736 fighters and 1,688 bombers, but the Luftwaffe only assessed 2,800 of them to be operational. The Luftwaffe's intelligence suggested that the Red Air Force had 15,000 pilots and 150,000 ground support and aircrew. Whilst the Luftwaffe had good intelligence on the I-16 fighter it was not so familiar with the newer Yaks and MiGs or the rate at which the Red Air Force was being re-equipped.

It was clear that the Luftwaffe was a finely tuned war machine equipped with first-class fighters and bombers, but one nagging doubt in the summer of 1941 was, would it be sufficient to overwhelm the largest air force in the world? The coming battle was certainly no foregone conclusion, as both sides had amassed considerable combat experience in the preceding years. What was clear to Göring and the Luftwaffe was that the first few days, if not the opening minutes, of Barbarossa would be crucial in destroying the Red Air Force wholesale.

This was how the Luftwaffe's pilots liked to view themselves – tough and confident. Prior to Hitler's invasion of the Soviet Union the Luftwaffe gained invaluable experience in the Spanish Civil War and during the blitzkrieg in the West. The second man is a Leutnant, or pilot officer.

A smiling Messerschmitt Bf 109 aircraftsman. On 22 June 1941, about 480 German fighters helped smash Stalin's air force in a single day. Luftwaffe losses were minimal.

The Luftwaffe's jewel in the crown in 1941 was undoubtedly the Messerschmitt Bf 109, which provided the mainstay of the Luftwaffe's fighter squadrons throughout the war. It first flew in 1935, with the Bf 109F appearing in May 1941.

The Focke-Wulf Fw 190 did not go into service until after Hitler's invasion of the Soviet Union. When it appeared in the autumn of 1941, thanks to its performance and agility it soon became known as the 'Butcher Bird'. Its one-piece rearward sliding canopy gave good all-round visibility and its wide-track undercarriage meant it could operate from rough airstrips, making it ideal for the Eastern Front.

The twin-engine Messerschmitt Bf 110 proved to be a failure as an escort fighter but a highly successful night fighter. Just over fifty were committed to the opening attacks on the Soviet Union. The following year most Bf 110 units were withdrawn to defend Germany and those that remained acted in a reconnaissance role.

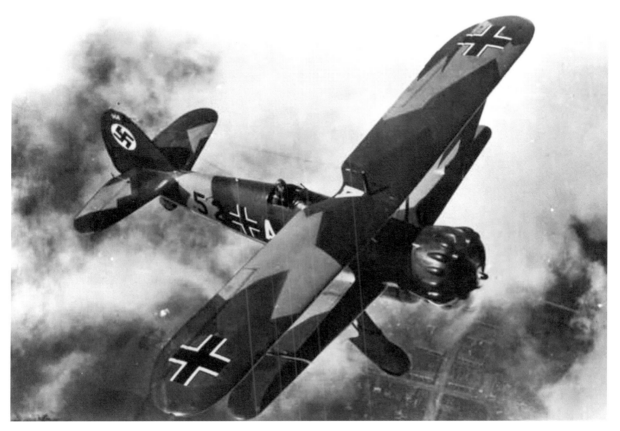

The Luftwaffe's key *Sturzkampfflugzeug*, or dive-bombers, consisted of the Henschel 123, pictured here, and the Junkers Ju 87. However, the Hs 123 performed better in ground attack than dive-bombing. It was the Luftwaffe's last operational biplane and remained on the Eastern Front until 1944.

Although the term *Sturzkampfflugzeug* covered all German aircraft with a dive-bombing capability the abbreviation Stuka became forever associated with the Ju 87 in the same way that the Soviet Il-2 became known as the Shturmovik. As a weapon of the blitzkrieg it was formidable and any lack of accuracy was made up for as a terror weapon.

The Luftwaffe's bomber force comprised the Dornier Do 17, Heinkel 111 and Junkers Ju 88. Although the Do 17 seen here saw action during the invasion of the Soviet Union most had been withdrawn from service by late 1941 as the aircraft quickly became obsolescent, having already suffered heavy losses in the battles of France and Britain.

The Heinkel He 111H formed the backbone of the Luftwaffe's bomber force from 1940 to 1943. Standard crew of the 111H was five, consisting of pilot, navigator/bombardier and three gunners, one of whom also served as the radio operator. Its limited manoeuvrability restricted its tactical support to the army so it was assigned a train-busting role on the Eastern Front. The He 111 was also used as a transport aircraft to keep the German Army supplied.

In contrast, the Junkers Ju 88 bomber proved to be one of the Luftwaffe's most versatile aircraft and was deployed in a wide variety of roles. Total Ju 88 production amounted to 14,676 aircraft, of which some 3,900 were fighter or ground-attack variants.

Luftwaffe ground crew haul a large bomb toward a Heinkel He 111, which already has its engines running ready for a sortie. Such large bombs were carried externally on this type of bomber, employing a rack underneath the bomb bay.

Luftwaffe ground crew servicing the two-seat Henschel Hs 126 reconnaissance aircraft. This provided the army's eyes in the sky. Just over 600 of these aircraft were built but were progressively replaced from 1942 by the twin-engine Focke-Wulf Fw 189.

Surplus Luftwaffe personnel such as these aircraftsmen would prove a major headache as the war progressed and a source of friction with the army.

Chapter Four

Catastrophic Summer

The Soviet Western Special Military District, just before 0045 hours on Sunday, 22 June 1941, received a warning from Generals Timoshenko and Zhukov. It read: 'A surprise attack by the Germans on the fronts of Leningrad, Baltic, Western Special, Kiev Special and Odessa Military districts is possible during the course of 22–23 June 1941. The mission of our forces is to avoid proactive actions of any kind. … At the same time, the … districts' forces are to be at full combat readiness to meet a surprise blow by the Germans or their allies.' Red Air Force pilots continued to sleep, their aircraft lined up on the airfields wingtip to wingtip.

At 0330 hours on the morning of 22 June 1941, the Luftwaffe spearhead attacked ten Soviet forward airfields. The raids, conducted by Do 17Zs, Ju 88s and He 111s, took the Red Air Force completely by surprise. Having had no warning, dazed and bleary-eyed pilots and ground crew, with bombs falling all around them, staggered from their billets. By the end of the day at least sixty-six Soviet airfields had been hit, and these had held 75 per cent of their fighter force.

A hail of fragmentation bombs fell on the Red Air Force's runways, taxiing strips and hangers. Soviet aircraft were either destroyed on the ground or shot out of the air. The Polikarpov I-153 and I-16 and the MiG-3, which formed the mainstay of the Soviet fighter squadrons, were simply no match for the Luftwaffe's fighters. Row upon row of Soviet aircraft were bombed and strafed where they stood. Some pilots managed to reach their aircraft and rose to meet their attackers but the battle was largely a one-sided massacre.

'It was on early Sunday morning, and many of the men were out on a leave pass,' recalled Colonel Vanyushkin, commander of the 23rd Air Division. 'Our airfields lay far too close to the frontier, and their positions were perfectly well known to the Germans. Furthermore, many regiments were just re-equipping with new types of aircraft, even on operational airfields. With proverbial Russian negligence both old and new types stood all about in uncamouflaged rows.'

Soviet troop concentrations were then bombed and strafed as they sought to mass in order to conduct counter-attacks against Hitler's blitzkrieg. On the day of the invasion German aircraft bombing Lvov airport also struck the barracks of the

32nd Tank Division, a key unit designated for the counter-attack. Luftflotte 2 set about Soviet railways, trains and bridges. The Red Army was paralysed by Hitler's version of 'shock and awe'.

Only at Boushev, near Stanislavov, did the Luftwaffe's Ju 88s suffer any notable casualties, losing nine aircraft. This trend was not repeated elsewhere. At Boushev, half of the sixty-six I-153s were lost on the ground and three were shot down tackling the bombers. Likewise, twenty-one MiG-3s were destroyed at the same airfield. A number of Soviet pilots claimed multiple kills elsewhere but there was no way of verifying the figures. There were fifteen reports of Soviet pilots deliberately ramming their adversaries in desperation. At the same time there were reports of Soviet fighter pilots shooting at their own side in the confusion.

Stalin's key Western Military District, containing eleven air divisions and twenty-six airfields, lost 387 fighters and 351 bombers from their 1,560 aircraft (of which 1,086 were serviceable). The three air divisions hit the hardest were the 9th, 10th and 11th Composite Air divisions supporting the 3rd, 4th and 10th armies in the frontier zone: the 9th lost 347 of its 409 aircraft; the 10th, 180 out of 231; and the 11th, 127 out of 199 aircraft. By the time the last German bomber was heading home these three Red Air Force units had been reduced from 839 to just 185 planes.

Further south, twenty-three airfields of Ukraine's Kiev Military District were also bombed at dawn and 277 aircraft destroyed. Lörzer's 2nd Air Corps, supporting Army Group Centre, claimed the destruction of 915 Soviet aircraft from 22 June to 26 July 1941. By the end of August, the Luftwaffe's score had risen to 2,606, almost half of which had been caught on the ground.

Those Red Air Force units in the Baltic Military District were not spared either. By 23 August, Förster's 1st Air Corps, supporting Army Group North, claimed 2,541 Soviet aircraft, 1,594 of which had been destroyed during strikes on airfields. Way to the south, the Luftwaffe enjoyed the least success against the Odessa Military District. More than a hundred of the district's 827 combat aircraft were the new MiG-3 fighters and these were able to oppose Greim's 5th Air Corps. The destruction of forty German aircraft for the loss of twenty-three Soviet fighters was claimed on the first day of the war. Captain Afanasy Karmanov of the 4th Fighter Regiment was credited with having destroyed two Ju 88 bombers and three Bf 109 fighters in his MiG-3 before being shot down and killed on the morning of 23 June.

The new Soviet aircraft types caused Red Air Force pilots recognition problems. It was in the Odessa Military District that Senior Lieutenant Pokryshkin, a Zveno leader in the 55th Fighter Regiment and later famed as the second-highest scoring Soviet fighter ace, made ready his MiG-3 for his very first kill. Unfortunately, he swooped down on a Red Air Force Su-2 dive-bomber, part of a unit en route to bomb German forces crossing the Pruth. This was a type of aircraft he had never seen before and assumed it was German until, as he closed in, he spotted the red stars on its fuselage.

By dusk Moscow admitted losses of 1,136 aircraft, of which just 336 had been brought down during aerial combat; the rest had been caught on the ground. These figures had risen to 4,017 aircraft by the end of the first week of fighting. For Stalin and the Red Air Force this was a disaster of titanic proportions. Rather improbably, Moscow claimed 244 German aircraft in the first twenty-four hours – Luftwaffe figures recorded the loss of just fifty-nine aircraft, rising to 150 by the end of the first week.

In the opening days of the Luftwaffe's attacks the Red Air Force's losses were largely obsolescent fighter planes caught on the taxi and runways rather than aircrews. Therefore, whilst many of the fighter and ground-attack pilots escaped, the bomber crews flying to try to stem the tide suffered heavily. The Red Air Force did everything it could to strike back at the Nazi invaders. After losing many of their fighters in the opening raids, bomber counter-attacks commenced on the afternoon of 22 June, concentrating on German columns and river crossings.

Soviet SB bombers, flying largely without fighter escort, were shot to pieces by prowling Bf 109s and flak as they approached their targets in level formations as if on training missions. Despite heavy losses the bomber crews kept up their attacks with formations of up to sixty aircraft. Initially, bomb loads were dropped from the regulation heights of 2,000 to 3,000 metres, but these were found to be ineffectual so raids were carried out as low as 600 metres, making the bombers sitting ducks. Many Luftwaffe pilots, while enjoying the ease of these 'turkey shoots', were horrified by the sacrifice of the Soviet bomber force in such an uneven battle.

In desperation, Red Air Force fighter pilots resorted to ramming – a tactic known as *taran*. In the Western Military District at 0430 hours on 22 June, Lieutenant Kokorev of the 124th Fighter Regiment took off with twenty-eight fighters. After exhausting his ammunition he rammed a Bf 110 and managed to make a forced landing after the German plane plummeted out of control. Just an hour later, Junior Lieutenant Butelin rammed a Ju 88 at low level over the Kiev Military District. At the same time, Senior Lieutenant Ivanov, a Zveno leader with the 46th Fighter Regiment, following five sorties and four fruitless combats flew his I-16 into the rear of a He 111 bomber, losing his life in the process. The tail of the Heinkel was torn off, with deadly results for the crew.

On 27 June, Junior Lieutenant Zdorovtsev, piloting an I-16 of the 158th Fighter Regiment on the North-Western Front, rammed a Ju 88 and parachuted to safety. Two fellow pilots followed his example and each claimed a German bomber in exchange for their I-16. West of Moscow, Junior Lieutenant Talalikhin on the night of

7/8 August rammed a crippled He 111 and parachuted from his I-16. 'I managed to hit the bomber's port engine and it turned away, losing height,' reported Talalikhin. 'It was at that moment my ammunition ran out and it struck me that, although I could still overtake it, it would get away. There was only one thing for it – to ram. If I'm killed, I thought, that's only one, but there are four fascists in the bomber.'

He was decorated a Hero of the Soviet Union the very next day, although by this stage *taran* had lost its novelty. While these tactics proved fruitful it took a special kind of courage to hope that after a deliberate collision the attacking pilot could jump clear or make a crash-landing.

Harald Henry, a 20-year-old German soldier, saw the power of the Luftwaffe on 25 June 1941. 'The sight of the line of retreat of their army, wrecked by our tanks and our Stukas, is truly awful and shocking. Huge craters left by our Stuka bombs all along the edges of the road that had blown even the largest and heaviest of their tanks up in the air and swivelled them round.'

By September 1941, Soviet aviation losses had reached an estimated 7,500 aircraft. These illustrated not only the inferiority of Soviet aircraft but also the poor training of its pilots. In addition, spares and replacement aircraft soon became a problem as the aviation factories were uprooted and their assembly lines were evacuated beyond the Ural Mountains. It left the Red Army undefended, and it was to be similarly crushed by the Wehrmacht.

Stalin knew that the Luftwaffe would soon blitz Moscow so aircraft were redirected from the other hard-pressed fronts to defend the capital. The lessons of Hitler's blitz on London did not go unheeded and extensive preparations were made. General Gromadin, the commander of the Moscow Air Defence Zone, had at his disposal Colonel Klimov's newly formed 6th PVO Fighter Corps, with almost 600 fighters plus the 1st PVO Anti-Aircraft Artillery Corps with 796 76mm and 85mm anti-aircraft guns. The Moscow Metro stations were readied as air-raid shelters and decoy fires were lit on the approach of the enemy's bombers to lure them away. Fire-fighting teams were put together ready to tackle the inevitable blazes. In the air, Soviet bombers were tasked to lead the Luftwaffe astray and follow them back to their bases.

Stalin also ensured the fighters deployed to Moscow were state of the art. Over half of Klimov's force were modern types; by early July his command contained 585 fighters, consisting of 170 MiG-3, seventy-five LaGG-3 and ninety-five Yak-1 fighters, backed by 200 I-16 and forty-five I-153. These were to be later bolstered by British-supplied Hurricanes and American-supplied P-40s. Up to 2,000 Soviet fighters took part in the defence of Moscow from July 1941 to January 1942. This meant that each of the four sectors of the Moscow PVO zone were protected by the equivalent of a fighter corps whilst the 6th PVO Fighter Corps was more the size of an air army.

The Western sector of the Moscow PVO under Colonel Stefanovski consisted of eleven fighter regiments. Of these only two were equipped with the outdated I-153 and I-16 fighters. Of the remaining nine, four had Yak-1s, two MiG-3s, two Hurricanes and one LaGG-3s, while a twelfth regiment was in reserve with P-40s. Colonel Trifonov's Southern sector was roughly the same, but smaller resources were committed to Colonels Mitenkov's and Yakushin's Northern and Eastern sectors.

Luftwaffe bombers, totalling 127 aircraft, first hit Moscow on the night of 21/22 July 1941, when four waves dropped 104 tons of high explosives and 46,000 incendiary bombs over five and a half hours. The results were poor and Soviet anti-aircraft guns claimed ten bombers, while another twelve fell victim to Soviet night fighters such as Pe-3s operating with searchlight batteries. The German bomber crews had been dazzled by more than 300 searchlights and their incendiary bombs failed to penetrate the roof of the Kremlin. The following night, Moscow was attacked by 115 bombers and then 100, but the Luftwaffe had greater priorities and the numbers after that declined to fifty, thirty and then just fifteen. Of the seventy-six raids on the city that year, forces ranging from just three to ten bombers conducted fifty-nine of these.

The Luftwaffe's 2nd Air Fleet soon found the weather a problem and by mid-November realized its temporary airfields were all but inoperable. The Luftwaffe's ground crews found their flesh sticking to the frozen airframes as well as their tools. Their aircrafts' liquid-fuelled engines refused to start as the temperatures plummeted.

The Red Air Force did its utmost to ignore the weather and from 15 November to 5 December 1941, clocked up 15,840 sorties. This equated to nearly five times the flying rates of the Luftwaffe. The 6th PVO Fighter Corps gave the Luftwaffe a tough time in the skies around Moscow. During the last two months of 1941 it claimed to have shot down 250 German planes. It was then the German Army's turn to be on the receiving end of things when the corps switched from its air defence role to ground attack and set about the German armies west of Moscow. Nevertheless, in total, from June to December 1941, the Soviets lost 21,200 aircraft, of which only about half were destroyed in combat.

The blazing remains of a Red Air Force biplane. At 0330 hours on the morning of Sunday, 22 June 1941, the Luftwaffe attacked ten Soviet forward airfields. Although an attack was anticipated the Red Air Force was caught completely unprepared.

A burning building in eastern Poland. Soviet barracks, hangers and runways were all systematically bombed, catching much of the Red Air Force asleep and off guard.

The devastated remains of a Soviet base. By the end of the day on 22 June 1941, at least sixty-six Soviet airfields had been hit and the Red Air Force's infrastructure lay smashed. Deprived of air support the Red Army very quickly suffered a similar fate as it was driven back and surrounded by the Wehrmacht.

In the vanguard of the air raids were Hitler's deadly Ju 87 Stukas, which delivered 250kg or 500kg bombs and strafed targets with their two wing-mounted 7.92mm machine guns. Once the Soviet fighters had been neutralized they had free reign to attack Soviet troop columns.

As the day wore on, He 111s ranged further afield with attacks launched against the Red Air Force in the Western, Baltic, Kiev and Odessa military districts. Again with the Red Air Force all but wiped out on the ground they were able to operate largely with impunity.

Later in the day, the scale of the disaster became apparent. The bulk of the Red Air Force's fighters never got airborne, as the assorted I-153, U-2 and I-16 aircraft shown here testify. Many aircraft were lined up wing tip to wing tip, making the Luftwaffe's task that much easier.

More scrap metal – consisting largely of wrecked I-153 fighters – photographed at a captured Soviet airbase. A twin-engine bomber is just visible in the background.

This Polikarpov I-16 fighter appears to have nose-dived after trying to take off. In the opening days of the Luftwaffe's attacks the Red Air Force's largely obsolescent fighters were caught on the taxi and runways rather than in the air.

Another I-16 nose-down; the aircraft's undercarriage suspension was hard, causing the aircraft to bounce violently when landing or taking off from uneven ground. The majority of Soviet fighter pilots killed or captured in the first forty-eight hours of Hitler's invasion never actually got airborne.

This I-16 was caught on the ground and shot to pieces. By the end of the first day of the German invasion the Red Air Force had lost 1,136 aircraft, of which just 336 had been shot down, the rest having been caught on their airfields.

This *Chaika* was also caught still on the ground. As a result of combat in the Far East the I-153 was criticized for lacking sufficient protective armour for the pilot and the engine.

These two I-16s lie abandoned at the roadside. As both have their undercarriage extended it's quite possible that their pilots had attempted emergency landings once they realized they could not reach their airfields. If fuel was low they had little option but to put down at the soonest opportunity or bail out and hope for the best.

Once the Red Air Force had been destroyed, the Luftwaffe set about the Red Army's troop concentrations with devastating effect. This enabled the Wehrmacht to trap millions of Soviet troops in a series of vast pockets in Byelorussia and Ukraine. In the first shot the crew of this lorry futilely sort shelter underneath it. In the second, these infantrymen were caught in the open.

Not content with eliminating the Red Air Force and helping to trap the Red Army, the Luftwaffe first attacked Moscow on the night of 21/22 July and again on 22/23 July 1941, exactly a month after the invasion started.

A shot-down Soviet aircraft lies wheels up amidst the snow. The 6th Air Defence Fighter Corps did everything it could to protect Moscow during the winter of 1941–42.

As most of the Red Air Force's more modern fighters were deployed to defend Moscow the Il-2 ended up being used in a fighter role for which it was ill-suited. This early single-seat model was captured on the ground.

From June to December 1941, the Red Air Force lost a staggering 21,200 aircraft and it seemed inconceivable that it could continue offering resistance. Nevertheless, from 15 November to 5 December 1941, it still managed to fly 15,840 sorties, nearly five times the number that the Luftwaffe flew. Such courage and stubbornness did not bode well for the Nazis on the Eastern Front.

Chapter Five

Junkers to the Rescue

The three-engine Junkers Ju 52 transport aircraft started life in the early 1930s in a civil aviation role and became the workhorse of the German military. The Luftwaffe variant of the Ju 52 saw action in 1936, when twenty aircraft were deployed to ferry 10,000 Spanish Nationalist troops from Morocco to Spain. With the outbreak of the Second World War in 1939, the Luftwaffe took over Lufthansa's fleet of fifty-nine Ju 52/3ms and used them extensively in airborne assault operations and supply missions. At the time of the Norwegian operation in early 1941, the Luftwaffe had 571 Ju 52 transports available.

The Ju 52 could only manage 275km/h (171mph) and was defended by single dorsal and ventral position machine guns. As a result it was very vulnerable to air attack and flak; of a force of 493 aircraft, more than 270 were damaged or lost during the airborne invasion of Crete in 1941. Throwing a lifeline to the German Army trapped in North Africa proved equally costly and 100 were shot down in April 1943.

Following the Battle of Moscow, 3,500 German troops were trapped from 21 January to 5 May 1942 in the Kholm Pocket, south of Leningrad. A much larger pocket was also encircled at Demyansk, south-east of Lake Ilmen. Once it became apparent that Soviet field batteries and anti-aircraft guns made it impossible for transport aircraft to land, the garrison at Kholm had to be kept resupplied by the Luftwaffe using DFS 230 and Go 242 cargo gliders. When glider losses became unacceptable containers were dropped by parachute.

The situation at Demyansk was far more desperate. Four Soviet armies had breached the lines of the German 16th Army between Demyansk and Staraya Russa, trapping six divisions, numbering about 100,000 men. Colonel General Keller, commanding Luftflotte 1 at Ostrov, met with the Luftwaffe's chief of air transport, Colonel Fritz Morzik.

'To ferry a daily quota of 300 tons to Demyansk,' Morzik said, 'I need a standing force of at least 150 serviceable machines and we only have half that number. To double it you will have to draw on other fronts and drain the homeland of all available machines.' The Ju 52 transport units had a total of 220 aircraft but just a third were serviceable, so nowhere near enough for such an ambitious operation. Keller had little choice but to agree and send out a request for every available 'special purpose' unit. One such unit under Major Beckmann found itself redeployed from the deserts of North Africa to the snowstorms and 40 degrees below zero of the Eastern Front.

'Secondly,' added Morzik, 'to operate in winter needs more ground staff and better technical equipment. I require mobile workshops, vehicles to warm up the aero-engines and auxiliary starters.' This was a harder request to meet; the shortage of ground personnel often meant that crews had to service their own aircraft. Morzik knew that the severe weather was affecting everything from the engines to the fuel lines, hydraulics, instruments and radios, all of which required constant attention to keep an aircraft airworthy. In addition, taking off and landing was hampered by flat tyres – the result of brittle and cracked rubber. Along with his operations chief, Captain Wilhelm Metscher, Morzik oversaw the relief operation from Pleskau-South, already occupied by a bomber unit.

Luftwaffe transport units were gathered at Pskov, Korov'e Selo, Ostrov and Riga to shift the 300 tons of supplies a day from Germany and across Eastern Prussia in a fleet of old and converted transport aircraft. These included Ju 86, Junkers W 34 and Focke-Wulf Fw 58 Weihe.

The first flight of Ju 53/3m into Demyansk, a former advanced tactical 800-yard by 50-yard airfield, was made on 20 February 1942. Initially it was hoped that flights by low-level single aircraft or small formations would get through, but these were pounced on by patrolling Soviet fighter aircraft. In addition, at low level approaching aircraft had to run the gauntlet of a 55-kilometre flak corridor created by Soviet anti-aircraft artillery. The Luftwaffe then organized formations of twenty to thirty transports flying at 2,000 metres, where possible, with fighter escort.

In response, three fighter regiments with MiG-3, Yak-1 and Hurricane fighters were despatched by the 6th PVO Fighter Corps to shoot down the Ju 52s. They lay in wait over Demyansk and as the German transport aircraft came down singly to land, they attacked from astern. As soon as the escort fighters appeared the Soviet pilots would dart away. Rather surprisingly, they made no effort to attack the supply bases outside the pocket.

Despite the most appalling weather, prowling enemy fighters and flak for three months – from 20 February to 19 May 1942 – the six trapped German divisions were kept alive thanks to the bravery of the Luftwaffe's transport pilots. They delivered a total of 24,303 tons of supplies and 5 million gallons of petrol. In addition, 22,093 wounded were flown out of the Demyansk Pocket and 15,446 replacements flown in.

From the Luftwaffe's standpoint, supplying Demyansk by air had been a success but it had come at a terrible cost. Whilst an average of 276 tons a day had been flown into the pocket, some 265 valuable Ju 52 transports and 383 crew had been lost. The latter was a particular blow: experienced aircrews had been expended and the pilot training programme was disrupted because instructors had been used to fly on the extensive supply route. The Ju 52 losses amounted to more than half the total production of the aircraft for 1941. At the same time those aircraft that had survived had been damaged in taxiing accidents on the frozen runways, engines had been pushed to their limit, and hydraulic systems and tyres worn out. The success at Demyansk convinced Hitler that he could rely on his air force to rescue the army whenever need be. Less than a year later at Stalingrad, this conviction would cost the Luftwaffe and the Wehrmacht dearly.

Under P.S. Stepanov, the 102nd Fighter Aviation Division initially defended Stalingrad. Stepanov's command consisted of eighty fighters, most of which were either the obsolescent I-15 or the outgunned and underpowered I-16. To try to compensate for this he requested a regiment of Yak-1s. General Novikov, responsible for air force planning and operations, despatched a regiment from Moscow equipped with Yak-7bs and Yak-9s.

The Battle of Stalingrad signalled the slow process of the Soviet Air Force wrestling air superiority from the Luftwaffe. By the winter of 1942 it was reorganized, equipped with new aircraft and had a good cadre of combat-experienced pilots. Stalingrad preceded the battle over the Kuban River in the spring of 1943 and was followed by the decisive blow against the Wehrmacht at Kursk. The Red Air Force, like the Luftwaffe before it during the Battle of Britain, soon learned that fighter-to-fighter combat was not very productive. It was far better to hunt and destroy enemy bombers and reconnaissance aircraft. This development led to the Soviet *zasada*, or ambush tactic.

According to Soviet figures, by early November 1942 Luftwaffe strength on the Eastern Front totalled 3,500 combat aircraft. Soviet industrial muscle had ensured that by this stage the Red Army's massive losses had been made good and the Red Air Force had 4,500 combat aircraft. On top of this the Soviet high command had considerable reserves. As a result Stalin decreed that the time was right to strike back. When the Red Army launched its counter-offensive at Stalingrad in the winter of 1942, three powerful air armies supported it.

At 0630 hours on 19 November 1942, massed Soviet artillery opened up on the Romanian 3rd Army's positions as a prelude to trapping the Germans at Stalingrad. German dive-bomber pilot Hans Rudel, flying above the battlefield, witnessed its disintegration: 'What troops are those coming towards us? Masses of brown uniforms – are they Russians? No, Romanians. Some of them are even throwing away their rifles in order to be able to run faster … we have now reached our allies' artillery emplacements. The guns are abandoned not destroyed. The ammunition lies beside them.'

General Paulus' 6th Army had the choice of making a fighting retreat or allowing itself to become trapped between the Don and Volga rivers. Wanting to know what was happening, Lieutenant General Martin Fiebig, commanding the Luftwaffe's 8th Air Corps in the Stalingrad area, telephoned 6th Army's chief of staff, Major General Arthur Schmidt, with Paulus himself listening in.

'The C-in-C proposes to defend himself at Stalingrad,' responded Schmidt.

'And how do you intend to keep the Army supplied?' asked Fiebig.

'That will have to be done from the air,' came the reply.

'A whole army?' gasped Fiebig. 'But it's quite impossible! Just now our transport planes are heavily committed in North Africa. I advise you not to be so optimistic.' He then phoned his boss, Colonel General von Richthofen. He, in turn, phoned Hans Jeschonnek, the Luftwaffe's chief of general staff.

'You've got to stop it!' demanded Richthofen. 'In the filthy weather we have here there's not a hope of supplying an army of 250,000 men from the air. It's stark staring madness!'

Three days after the Soviet offensive started, they captured the Luftwaffe's airfield at Kalach as the two pincers of their offensive snapped shut. Predictably, the fighters of General Rudenko's 16th Air Army then set about the Luftwaffe's 200-mile air corridor to Stalingrad. In many cases the Luftwaffe's transport aircraft were sitting ducks; the Ju 52s, Ju 90s, Ju 290s, Fw 200s, He 111s and He 177s, often flown by experienced and irreplaceable instructors, were cut to pieces. For example, on 30 November, Colonel Kitayev's regiment from the 283rd Aviation Division pounced on seventeen Ju 52s and their escort of four Bf 109s. In the aerial melee that followed one Bf 109 was shot down along with five of the transports.

For the Luftwaffe, maintaining the air bridge was a disaster. During the eight weeks of the Soviet air blockade the Red Air Force claimed 676 transport aircraft, 227 bombers and 162 fighters. From 24 November 1942 to 31 January 1943, according to German sources the Luftwaffe lost 266 Ju 52s, 165 He 111s, forty-two Ju 86s, nine Fw 200s, seven He 177s and one Ju 290 – a total of 490 aircraft, which equated to more than an entire air corps. It was a blow from which the Luftwaffe never recovered.

Once the Romanian, Hungarian and Italian armies supporting the Germans at Stalingrad had been smashed the Luftwaffe's sacrifice was for nothing. Field Marshal von Paulus' 6th Army surrendered on 2 February 1943. For General Novikov it was vindication of his reorganization of the Red Air Force, the increasing proficiency of its pilots and the effectiveness of the new fighter designs.

By the end of Stalingrad, in total, 676 Ju 52s had been lost – more than 60 per cent of the total strength committed to the battle. Heavy losses of the Ju 52 on the Eastern Front meant production could not keep up with demand. In 1941, 451 were delivered, with more than 500 destroyed. As a result a production line was set up in France at the Amiot factory at Colombes, with subcontractors in the Paris area.

The first French-built Ju 52s were accepted in June 1942, with forty more delivered in the next six months and 321 the following year. Assembly was also arranged in Budapest from German sub-components and twenty-six were completed in January 1944. Of these, just four went to the Luftwaffe and the rest to the Hungarian Air Force. When production in France and Germany ended in mid-1944, a total of 4,845 Ju 52s had been produced. However, the Luftwaffe's transport units were already damaged beyond repair thanks to Stalingrad.

The Ju 52s resupplying German divisions at Demyansk averaged 276 tons a day by flying in formations of up to thirty aircraft at very low level. The cost of running the gauntlet of a 55km Soviet flak corridor was the loss of 383 air crew and 265 Ju 52s.

A three-engine Junkers Ju 52 takes to the skies. The Ju 52/3m transport aircraft threw a vital lifeline to German units trapped by the Red Army during 1942. It started out in a civil aviation role but proved its worth when Hitler ordered the Luftwaffe to ferry General Franco's Spanish Nationalist troops from Morocco to Spain at the start of the Spanish Civil War in 1936.

Luftwaffe personnel pose in front of a Ju 52. Prior to the campaign fought on the Eastern Front this aircraft suffered very heavy losses during the invasion of Crete, when it was used to deliver German airborne troops.

The Ju 52 also served in a medical evacuation role. Despite fierce opposition from three Soviet fighter regiments, Ju 52s miraculously managed to rescue more than 22,000 German wounded from the Demyansk Pocket as well as flying in almost 15,500 reinforcements during the winter of 1941–42.

German troops boarding a Gotha Go 242 glider at Kholm. The Luftwaffe resorted to gliders after transport could not get through; when glider losses mounted, the only option was container drops.

Camouflaged for winter operations this Ju 52 is bringing reinforcements to Demyansk.

A Stuka over Stalingrad. Thanks to Demyansk, Hitler mistakenly thought that the Luftwaffe would be able to keep the trapped 6th Army supplied at Stalingrad.

Russian civilians wander through the bomb-shattered remains of Stalingrad. This proved to be the turning point of the Luftwaffe's fortunes on the Eastern Front.

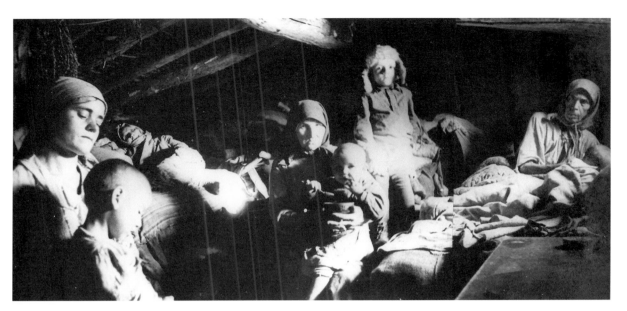

Russian women and children take shelter from the winter and the incessant raids conducted at Stalingrad.

While the air bridge to Demyansk from February to May 1942 had saved six German divisions, the Luftwaffe found it impossible to resupply an entire army at Stalingrad during the winter of 1942–43.

Aircraft such as the Ju 290 long-range bomber were pressed into service to try to maintain the ill-fated Stalingrad air bridge.

This air defence gunner keeps watch for Soviet air attacks on a Luftwaffe base. The air battle over Stalingrad proved particularly bloody.

Trying to keep the German 6th Army resupplied at Stalingrad cost 266 Ju 52 along with more than 200 other types of transport aircraft. It was a devastating blow to the Luftwaffe's transport units and Hitler never forgave Göring for this failure.

Russian civilians douse their homes following an air raid.

Wings from a Soviet aircraft make an impromptu windbreak.

The Soviet 16th Air Army did all it could to disrupt the Luftwaffe's air bridge; it also attacked targets within the Stalingrad Pocket and harried German forces trying to cut their way through on the ground. The German 6th Army was left with little option but surrender.

According to the Soviet caption, this is the engine from a Heinkel brought down in the Stalingrad area in early 1943 by a young fighter pilot called L. Tomalchen. The Luftwaffe was never really able to recover from its losses at Stalingrad.

Chapter Six

Circle of Death

Following the disastrous summer of 1941, General Aleksandr Novikov instigated a reorganization of the Red Air Force that in May 1942 witnessed the creation of independent air armies to replace the corps. These bigger formations consisted of five or more fighter aviation divisions, which offered a far greater punch. By 1944 these air armies included more than 1,000 fighters, bombers, ground-attack and reconnaissance aircraft. Also in 1942, in light of the German threat some forty fighter regiments were assigned to air defence. Until November 1942 the Red Air Force focused on rebuilding its ground-attack force in order to help stem the Nazi tide.

By far the best ground-attack weapon in the Soviet armoury was the famous Ilyushin 'Flying Tank', or Il-2 Shturmovik, which first appeared in 1941. This was designed as a low-level close-support aircraft capable of defeating enemy armour and other ground targets. Following early teething problems it developed into one of the world's most potent ground-attack aircraft, armed with 23mm or 37mm cannon, machine guns, rockets and bombs, including anti-tank bomblets. With good cause, the Germans dubbed it the *Schlächter* (slaughterer).

Il-2 pilots developed the 'Circle of Death' for attacking panzers. They would circle around the enemy armour and peel off to make individual attack runs. When the run ended, they would rejoin their formation to wait for another turn. This kept the Germans under constant fire for as long as the Il-2s had ammunition left. Notably, during the summer of 1943 and the Battle of Kursk the Shturmovik finally came into its own, severely mauling the 2nd and 3rd Panzer divisions.

To support Hitler's plans to smash the Red Army at Kursk, in the summer of 1943 the Luftwaffe massed everything it could spare to support Operation Citadel. General Hans Seidemann mustered 1,000 bombers, fighters, ground-attack and anti-tank aircraft in support of 4th Panzer Army's Southern Pincer. The Northern Pincer formed by 9th Army was allocated another 700 aircraft under Major General Paul Deichmann.

In the meantime, the Red Air Force, invigorated by its success at Stalingrad and growing proficiency, felt confident enough to try to pre-empt Hitler's offensive. Just as the Luftwaffe was about to take off from its five airfields around Kharkov on 5 July 1943, it discovered hundreds of enemy bombers bearing down on it. At the very point that Hitler's Operation Citadel was launched, the German Army almost lost its vital air support.

At the eleventh hour the Luftwaffe was warned by radio monitors who detected increased communication between the Soviet air regiments. Also, the radar stations at Kharkov reported large formations of enemy aircraft heading their way. These included 285 fighters and 132 Shturmoviks from the Soviet 2nd and 17th Air armies. Panic ensued on the crowded Kharkov airfields and the bombers' departure was postponed. The plan had been that they would take off first and gather over their bases to await their fighter escort.

Instead, German fighters at Mikoyanovka and Kharkov were scrambled and there followed the largest air battle of the war as they intercepted up to 500 Soviet fighters, ground-attack aircraft and bombers. General Seidemann reported, 'It was a rare spectacle; everywhere planes were burning and crashing. In no time at all some 120 Soviet aircraft were downed. Our own losses were so small as to represent total victory, for the consequence was complete German air control in the 8th Air Corps sector.'

This was a major setback, for the Red Air Force committing so many fighters to this abortive pre-emptive strike meant that it was unable to challenge Luftwaffe supremacy on the southern flank of the Kursk salient, and in the north its response to Luftwaffe attacks was often ineffectual. Certainly in the northern sector Soviet fighters only began to react to Citadel in the late afternoon and Fw 190s brought down 110 Soviet aircraft by nightfall. Thanks to the poor performance of the two fighter corps with responsibility for providing front-line cover, both had their commanders replaced immediately.

To make matters worse, initial Red Air Force tactics designed to stop Hitler's panzers were flawed. The Shturmoviks, armed with an array of cannon, rockets and anti-tank bombs, failed to get through. The Il-2s and Pe-2s were despatched in small groups lacking fighter escort and were easily picked off. This was soon remedied using regimental-size formations that were easier to escort and they broke through thanks to weight of numbers. Low-level bombing passes were abandoned in favour of dive-bombing at 1,000 metres at 30 or 40 degree angles. By 8 July, the German Army's advance at Kursk had slowed and the Luftwaffe's control over the battlefield was declining.

Supported by Gromov's 1st and Naumenko's 15th Air armies, a week later Zhukov launched his counter-offensive with the Western and Bryansk fronts. These were joined by Rudenko's 16th Air Army on 15 July, when the Central Front went over to the offensive. In just five days, the 15th Air Army flew some 4,800 sorties whilst the 16th managed over 5,000, more than half of which were conducted by Pe-2s and Shturmoviks against retreating German troops.

Fortunately for him the Luftwaffe ensured that Hitler's defeat at Kursk was not an even greater disaster than it could have been. On 8 July, Hs 129B-2s based at Mikoyanovka and commanded by Captain Bruno Meyer destroyed a Soviet armoured threat to 4th Panzer Army's exposed left flank. To the north of Kursk, as the German offensive ground to a halt the German Orel salient came under threat as the Red Army sought to surround 2nd Panzer Army. Thanks to the Luftwaffe they narrowly avoided a repeat of Kalach, when the German Army had been cut off at Stalingrad.

Alarmingly, by 19 July 1943, Soviet tanks had reached Khotinez, cutting the vital Bryansk–Orel railway. Stukas operating from Karachev, supported by other anti-tank planes, bombers and fighters, flew to the rescue. For the first time a Soviet armoured breakthrough imperilling the rear of two whole armies was driven back from the air. Although during 19–20 July the Luftwaffe's pilots prevented an even larger Stalingrad, this was to be its last major operation on the Eastern Front.

To the south the Red Army then sought to liberate Kharkov and the Red Air Force set about German armour, moving up to reinforce their defences. Kharkov was taken on 23 August and once the Kharkov airfields were lost the Luftwaffe withdrew to its bases at Dnepropetrovsk, Kremenchug and Mirgorod to help hold the Dnieper Line. It was once again spread over the whole front, providing direct support to the army. For the bombers, this was a death sentence.

During the last half of 1943, with about 8,500 aircraft Red Air Force numbers remained static, but over the first six months of 1944, it rapidly expanded to 13,500 planes. That year it introduced a new tactical bomber into service, the Tu-2, which was to play a key role in the Red Army's final offensives. In addition, by 1943–44 some 12,000 Il-2s were in service and the Soviets were flying the IL-2m3 variant, which included a rear gunner. Similarly, the improved La-5FN and Yak-3 fighters appeared in 1943, which helped the Red Air Force wrestle air superiority from the Luftwaffe. By May 1944, the Soviet fighter squadrons were being equipped with an improved version of the La-5, known as the La-7. The Soviets' dabbling with strategic bombers was half-hearted at best and dogged by engine problems. Production of the Pe-8 strategic bombers, which played a limited role at Kursk, was ended in 1944 after just seventy-nine had been built.

Britain and the Commonwealth supplied a total of 4,770 aircraft, whilst from 1942 until the end of the war America provided another 14,800, of which 9,438 were fighters. Stalin received new ground-attack aircraft in 1944 courtesy of the Americans, principally the Bell P-63 Kingcobra, an upgrade of the earlier P-39 Aircobra, the P-40 and the P-47. The Soviets received about 2,000 P-40s by March

1944, but they did not like them, considering them cast-offs, and the aircraft were largely relegated to training. Only 200 P-47s were sent during 1944–45; in contrast they received 2,421 P-63s, which were based on a proven and well liked design. The Soviets found the Aircobra, armed with a 37mm cannon, to be an excellent ground-attack aircraft. They nicknamed it *Britchik* (little shaver) and received 4,750 of these.

However, by this stage in the war the Soviets were keener on bombers and transports, as their factories were producing fighters equal or superior in quality and in plentiful numbers. During 1944 aircraft production reached 40,300 machines. To supplement the Soviet bomber force the Americans provided 2,908 A-20 Havoc light bombers and 862 B-25 Mitchell medium bombers.

By the time of Operation Bagration the Soviets had got the hang of their American-supplied fighters. Two years earlier, for fear of American spies or simply national pride, Stalin had refused offers of American pilots and mechanics. The results, as American journalist Walter Kerr recalled, were predictable:

> One result was that in the early months when they used our Aircobras and B-25 medium bombers, many were damaged through inexperienced handling. Both planes have a nose wheel, which has led to their being called planes with a tricycle landing gear. In fact, they should be landed on two wheels, then nosed over on to the front wheel as the pilot taxis across the field. The Russians, however, tried to land them on three wheels, and the relatively weak forward wheel frequently broke.

The Americans secured agreement with Stalin for their air force to operate from the Soviet Union in 1944. Apart from the RAF fighter squadron based at Murmansk to help protect the Arctic convoys, this was Stalin's only concession to the Western Allies' desire to operate from his territory.

Nikita Khrushchev recalled:

> I got my first glimpse of Americans in the late spring or early summer of 1944 near Kiev. It was a bright, warm day. Suddenly we heard a rumbling noise in the distance. We scanned the sky and saw a large formation of airplanes flying toward us. I'd never seen this type of plane before. I realized they must be Americans because we didn't have anything like them in our own air force. I certainly hoped they were American; the only other thing they could have been was German. I later found out that these planes were B-17 'flying fortresses' and were based outside Poltava as part of our agreement with [President] Roosevelt.

Dubbed Operation Frantic, the Americans had considerable expectations of this shuttle bombing of Germany. However, the success was short-lived thanks to the Luftwaffe. Khrushchev noted: 'Somehow the Germans were able to track the American bombers back to Poltava and bomb their base. I received a report that many planes had been destroyed and many lives had been lost. Most of the casualties were our own men whom we had provided as maintenance personnel at the base.'

This retaliatory raid took place on 21–22 June 1944. Only eighteen American missions were flown, the whole operation largely being stymied by Stalin, who suspected American motives.

Despite its shortcomings the I-16 was flown by a number of Soviet aces, including Senior Lieutenant A.G. Lomokin, Captain B.F. Safonov and Senior Lieutenant M. Vasiliev. In 1943 it was still in service as a fighter-bomber, but its speed put it at a disadvantage when faced with faster and more manoeuvrable enemy fighters. Losses of I-16 at Kursk ensured it was subsequently withdrawn from operational service.

The Lavochkin La-5 fighter was first tested operationally over Stalingrad by a specially formed trials regiment in September 1942. They found it a vast improvement over the much maligned LaGG-3; early combats showed it to have a better all-round performance than the Bf 109G, except its climb rate was not as good. To remedy this shortcoming the modified La-5FN appeared in March 1943 and helped the Red Air Force establish air superiority for the first time.

The Junkers Ju 87 G-2 was nicknamed the *Panzerknacker* (tank cracker) or *Kanaonenvogel* (cannon bird) and was armed with a pair of under-wing Flak 18 37mm cannon with twelve rounds per gun. This proved capable of destroying all but the heaviest Soviet tanks with its tungsten-cored rounds. Even the Soviet T-34 medium tank was not immune to the G-2.

A German bomber pilot scans the skies; a sudden speck on the horizon would lead to chatter on the radio, warning the gunners they were under attack. By 1943, the Luftwaffe's twin-engine bombers were very vulnerable to enemy fighters when flying without escort.

A flight of Il-2 Shturmoviks. The two-seat variant first appeared over Stalingrad at the end of October 1942. The following year, the Il-2M was produced armed with 23mm cannon and the Il-2m3 with 37mm cannon. On 5 July 1943, a force of 132 Shturmoviks – part of a fleet of 500 aircraft – launched a surprise attack on the Luftwaffe's airfields around Kharkov.

What appears to be the remains of a Soviet SB-2 bomber. An upgraded variant was the SB-2bis, which had up-rated engines and greater fuel capacity. The Luftwaffe was forewarned of the Red Air Force's attack at Kharkov and managed to shoot down 120 aircraft.

German troops pose on a crashed single-seat Il-2. The large undercarriage fairings on the wings left the retracted undercarriage partially exposed, but meant the pilot could make a belly-up landing without too much harm to the aircraft. In this instance the propeller and the wing have been damaged; the bent propeller props indicate the engine was still running when it hit the ground.

A tail section is all that remains of this obliterated bomber. The loss of so many aircraft from the Soviet 2nd and 17th Air armies on 5 July 1943 in the pre-emptive strike on the Luftwaffe at Kharkov meant the Red Air Force was unable to challenge Luftwaffe superiority over the Kursk salient during the opening stages of Hitler's Operation Citadel.

Little remains of this Il-2 – the circular metal tube projecting from the propeller spinner is not a weapon, rather a starter dog used for turning and firing the engine in the same way as a vehicle starting handle.

A German souvenir hunter collects the remains of a Soviet aircraft that came down in some woods. The splintered trees were probably a result of the crash.

Heinkel He III bombers were deployed to support Hitler's Operation Citadel but they proved vulnerable to Soviet Yaks and MiGs.

Introduced in 1942, the German Henschel Hs 129, armed with a 30mm cannon, like the Ju 87G-2 was nicknamed the *Panzerknacker* (tank cracker) but was never available in sufficient numbers as only 865 were ever built. Nonetheless, on 8 July 1943, HS 129s played a key role in defending the 4th Panzer Army's exposed flank.

Likewise, on 19 July 1943, Stukas helped prevent the German 2nd Panzer Army from being surrounded in the Orel salient.

Although the Henschel Hs 123A biplane was obsolescent it remained in service on the Eastern Front until 1944. The Hs 123C variant was armed with a 20mm cannon.

A Russian cornfield became the last resting place for this Il-2. In the opening stages of Citadel Shturmovik tactics proved flawed. Initially, the Il-2s and Pe-2s flew in small groups without fighter cover and proved easy pickings for enemy fighters. Once the formations were beefed up they were able to fight their way through and dive-bomb the panzers.

Another Shturmovik that came down on the Russian Steppe.

The Red Air Force received both British and American aircraft, including this Hurricane. The Soviet officer on the left is watching the RAF pilot getting into his parachute.

This Russian house had a near miss judging by the wreckage of this Soviet aircraft.

The Ju 87 was also operated by the other Axis allies, including the Bulgarian, Hungarian and Romania air forces.

A heavily touched up Soviet propaganda shot showing Shturmoviks attacking a column of panzers. The wartime caption reads, 'Soviet attack planes annihilating a German tank column'.

Chapter Seven

Heroes of the Soviet Union

The term 'ace' was first officially used by the Soviets in December 1941 to describe a pilot with three or more confirmed kills. This was revised by the end of the following year to at least ten, which earned the pilot the Gold Star of the Hero of the Soviet Union. They were used as morale boosters and their names and exploits were made public by Stalin's propaganda machine.

Ivan Kozhedub, with sixty-two enemy aircraft downed, became the highest scoring Allied pilot of the Second World War. At least six other pilots – Grigori Rechkalov, Aleksandr Pokryshkin, Nikolai Gulayev, Kirill Yevstigneyev, Nikolai Skomorokhov and possibly Nikolai Shutt – are believed to have scored fifty or more. Vladimir Lavrinenkov claimed some twenty-three and Vladimir Orekhov nineteen personal and three group kills. The confirmation process was quite stringent, requiring proof from two other pilots involved, from ground troops, partisans or verification on recaptured territory. The decision to confirm personal or group kills varied from unit to unit, and some group kills were deemed personal, with the lead attacker getting the credit.

Flying the La-5FN and the La-7, Kozhedub clocked up his impressive total after flying 326 operational sorties and engaging in 126 combats. All of his victories were against conventional piston-engined aircraft, with the exception of one Me 262 jet fighter. His exploits were widely reported and he was awarded the Hero of the Soviet Union three times. He survived the war and went on to fly over Korea in the early 1950s.

Rechkalov, although accused of being a dangerous glory hunter by fellow ace and superior officer Pokryshkin, was involved in 122 air battles, during which his total reached fifty-six personal and five group victories. Despite being relieved of his command for failing to support his comrades in air-to-air combat he was awarded the Hero of the Soviet Union twice and survived the war.

Pokryshkin graduated from the Kacha Air Force Pilots' School in 1939 and went on to fly more than 600 sorties. He fought in 156 air engagements, achieving fifty-nine kills, including up to six group kills. He initially flew the troublesome MiG-3, followed by the Yak-1 and then the lend-lease P-39 and P-63. He saw action on the opening day of the war and in May 1944 was appointed commander of the 9th Guards Fighter Aviation Division, seeing combat on the Caucasus and Ukrainian fronts. He survived the war and was awarded Hero of the Soviet Union on three occasions.

In June 1941 Boris Safonov was commanding a squadron of I-16s. He then became one of four Northern Fleet pilots to convert to the British Hurricane and served as an instructor for Soviet pilots assigned to the aircraft. The first double Hero of the Soviet Union winner, Safonov was the first Soviet fighter ace to achieve twenty-four personal kills and fourteen group kills, before being killed in his P-40 on 30 May 1942. On his last mission he destroyed three Ju 88s before being hit and ditching in the sea.

Nelson Gevorgovich Stepanyan was a Soviet Shturmovik fighter ace who was dubbed the 'Storm Petrel of the Baltic Sea'. Before his death in 1944 he conducted 239 combat missions and in that time destroyed 600 armoured vehicles, eighty tanks, fifty-three ships and twenty-seven aircraft, which was quite a tally by anyone's reckoning.

Stepanyan was in fact not Russian or Ukrainian, but an Armenian, having been born in Shusha, Elisabethpol Governorate in 1913, although his family moved to Yerevan, the Armenian capital, when he was young. He studied at military school and went on to become a flight instructor at the Bataisk Naval Aviation School in the mid-1930s. When Hitler attacked the Soviet Union Stepanyan was instructing at another flight academy.

In response to this assault on his motherland Stepanyan volunteered for active duty. He was assigned as a pilot to a Ilyushin Il-2 fighter-bomber squadron deployed in the Baltic region. Serving with the 2nd Air Squadron, 8th Air Brigade, 57th Division he was involved in the battles to defend Leningrad, which was soon besieged by the Germans and Finns. By November 1942, Stepanyan was reported to have single-handedly knocked out seventy-eight enemy trucks, sixty-seven tanks, sixty-three anti-aircraft guns, thirty-six railroad cars, twenty merchantmen and warships (including a destroyer), nineteen mortars, thirteen fuel tankers, twelve armoured cars, seven long-range guns, five ammunition dumps and five bridges.

The following year he was promoted to the rank of major and took command of the 47th Fighter Division. They supported the Soviet offensives in the Crimea around Sevastopol, Sudak and Theodosia. For their heroic exploits against the German and Romanian forces in the Crimea Stepanyan's formation was redesigned the Guards 47th Theodosia Fighter Division.

In May, Stepanyan and his triumphant division returned to the Baltic Front to fight against the Germans and their Finnish allies. He had on one occasion been shot down behind enemy lines, but by good fortune fell in with Soviet partisans who escorted him back to Soviet lines so that he could resume his part in the air war. His luck ran out on 14 December 1944, when he was on patrol over Liepāja, Latvia. His aircraft was hit by anti-aircraft fire and he died crashing his plane into a German warship.

His pilots were so devastated by his loss that they wrote to his parents saying, 'We all wept when Nelson Gevorgovich failed to return on that fateful day. They say that tears bring comfort. But the few tears of a soldier, like the red-hot drops of metal, burn the heart and call for vengeance.' Stepanyan was awarded the highest honour with the title of Hero of the Soviet twice, the second time posthumously. He also gained the Order of Lenin twice and the Order of the Red Banner three times.

At the onset of the Second World War, whilst there were no formal restrictions on women serving in combat roles with the Soviet armed forces, initially the Soviet authorities did all they could to discourage them. Despite this, women did become fighter and bomber pilots flying with the Red Air Force. Marina Mikhailovna Raskova is known as the Russian Amelia Earhart because of her civilian flying exploits. In 1933 she was the first woman to become a navigator in the Red Air Force and during the war she formed three all-female aviation regiments (the 586th, 587th and 588th).

It is said that Raskova used her connections with Stalin to get women accepted as combat pilots. She commanded the 587th Bomber Aviation Regiment (also known as the 125th Guards Bomber Aviation Regiment), which flew the Petlyakov Pe-2 twin-engine dive-bomber. This caused resentment amongst many male pilots operating obsolete aircraft. Tragically, Raskova was killed making a forced landing on 4 January 1943.

The first all-female unit to take part in combat was the 586th Fighter Aviation Regiment, which went into battle on 16 April 1942. It was involved in 125 air battles and shot down thirty-eight enemy aircraft. They operated the Yak-1, which appeared in 1940 and led to the more successful Yak-1M and Yak-7A. Yekaterina Vasylievna Budanova, who was credited with eleven victories, along with Lydia Litvyak became one of the world's first female fighter aces.

After working in an aircraft factory in Moscow, Budanova became a flight instructor in the late 1930s and took part in several air parades flying the single-seat Yakolev UT-1. After the German attack she joined the air force and was assigned to the 586th Fighter Regiment.

Piloting the Yak-1, Budanova flew her first combat missions over Saratov in April 1942. That September, along with Lydia Litvyak, Maria M. Kuznetsova and Raisa Beliaeva, she was sent to join the 437th Fighter Regiment based on the east bank of the Volga. There they were involved in the Battle of Stalingrad.

Because the 437th was operating the LaGG-3 fighter, its commander, Major

Khvostikov, was sceptical about the women's capabilities. He was soon proved wrong and on 14 September 1942, Budanova and Litvyak shot down a Bf 109. Budanova then achieved her first solo kill on 6 October, when she claimed a Junkers Ju 88 bomber. Then, from October until January 1943, she and Litvyak fought with the 9th Guards Fighter Regiment in the Stalingrad area. This unit was made up of aces or potential aces. Initially the two women flew together but then operated separately as wingmen to male pilots.

In January 1943, the 9th Guards Fighter Regiment was re-equipped with American-supplied Bell P-39 Cobra, and Budanova and Litvyak were sent to the 296th Fighter Aviation Regiment so they could continue to fly Yaks. Budanova was awarded the Order of the Red Star on 23 February 1943. On the morning of 19 July 1943, she took off for an escort mission and near the city of Antracit in Luhansk Oblast became involved in a dogfight. Seeing three Messerschmitts going for the bombers she was escorting, Budanova attacked them, shooting down two. Wounded, and with her own plane on fire, she managed to land, but when some local farmers pulled her clear they found she had died of her injuries.

Budanova was twice awarded the Order of the Patriotic War, but it was not until 1993 that she was posthumously awarded the title Hero of the Russian Federation in lieu of the Hero of the Soviet Union. Lydia Litvyak also achieved about a dozen victories, but was killed shortly after her friend, on 1 August 1943. President Gorbachev posthumously awarded her the Hero of the Soviet Union on 6 May 1990.

The third all-female unit, the 46th Taman Guards Night Bomber Aviation Regiment, started life as the 588th Night Bomber Regiment. The practicalities of war meant that only the 588th remained all-female. Major Tamara Aleksandrovna Kazarinova, commanding the 586th, was replaced by a man in October 1942; likewise, after Raskova's, death a man took charge of the 587th. In addition, the top rear machine-gun position on the regiment's Pe-2 dive-bombers required someone tall; as not all the women met this criterion, men joined the crews as radio operators/tail gunners and flew with them.

The 588th Night Bomber Regiment flew with the 4th Air Army from June 1942. It was reorganized as the 46th Guards Night Bomber Aviation Regiment the following year and was then honoured with the title 'Taman' after taking part in the battle for the Taman Peninsula. In light of the regiment's U-2/Po-2 being a wood and canvas-built biplane, it did not seem best suited for modern aerial warfare or even being relegated to night raids. However, its maximum speed was slower than the stall speed of both the Bf 109 and the Fw 190, which made it difficult to shoot down. Also, to avoid flak and alerting the enemy on approach to target, they developed the tactic of idling the engine and gliding to bomb release point. This was particularly unnerving for those being bombed and led to the German nickname of Night Witches.

The Night Witches became the most highly decorated female unit, with twenty-three of its members being awarded the Hero of the Soviet Union. The regiment flew more than 23,000 sorties, dropping 3,000 tons of bombs for the loss of thirty crew. Each pilot flew more than 800 missions and often multiple ones; for example, Nadezhda Popova flew eighteen sorties in a single night.

This was how Soviet pilots liked to see themselves – cast in a heroic and dashing mould. This Yak pilot is L. Tomalchen, who was photographed in the Stalingrad Front in early 1943. He had just returned from combat involving seven enemy planes, during which he shot down a Heinkel and damaged a Ju 87.

Another pilot posing for the camera, this time with his Il-2. Ground-attack pilots produced aces as well as the fighter pilots; most notable was Nelson Stepanyan, who was credited with destroying an incredible 600 armoured vehicles, eighty tanks, fifty-three ships and twenty-seven aircraft. Not surprisingly, in light of his naval victories he was dubbed the 'Storm petrel of the Baltic Sea'.

Looking tough, cigarette between his lips, Aleksandr Pokryshkin was made a Hero of the Soviet Union on three separate occasions. He started the war flying the MiG-3, scoring almost twenty victories in this aircraft. Pokryshkin then converted to the Yak-1 and the Bell P-39 Aircobra. He refused to convert to the La-5 on grounds its firepower was insufficient. He also cancelled a conversion to the La-7, opting for the Bell P-63 Kingcobra. During his career he brought down fifty-nine enemy aircraft, although Pokryshkin himself put the figure at nearer 100.

Young Lydia Litvyak was the top female Soviet fighter pilot; she clocked up twelve solo victories and at least four shared kills during sixty-six combat missions. She was the first female fighter pilot to shoot down an enemy plane and the first female pilot to gain the title fighter ace. She was killed at the age of just twenty-one on 1 August 1943, during the Battle of Kursk. Her friend Yekaterina Budanova, credited with eleven victories, was killed on 19 July 1943.

Soviet ground crew preparing a Shturmovik for take-off. The two-seat Il-2M featured a rear-facing 12.7mm machine gun in a heavily armoured cockpit area in addition to the 23mm forward-firing cannon in the leading edges of the wings. Note the Polikarpov U-2/Po-2 biplane just visible in the background.

German troops examine early model single-seat Il-2s. The first aircraft appears to have crash-landed while the second one was abandoned after being damaged.

The Polikarpov U-2 (supplemented by the R-5 and R-Z) was widely used on the Eastern Front in a variety of roles. As a light bomber it proved vulnerable to enemy flak so in 1942 was deployed in a night bomber role. Its main claim to fame was with the all-female 588th Night Bomber Regiment nicknamed the Night Witches.

This Soviet armourer is arming the bomb load on a U-2. This aircraft could take six 50kg (110lb) bombs, which, delivered at night from low level, had a devastating effect on German morale.

This R-5 or R-Z fitted with skis for winter operations ended up upside down and was either shot down or suffered a take-off accident. The Red Air Force was equipped with some 5,000 R-5 and 1,000 R-Z. They could carry 250kg (550lb) and 400kg (882lb) of bombs respectively.

A portrait for the family extolling the virtues of the Il-2m3 and the U-2. The Soviets were quick to appreciate ground-attack aircraft.

Focke-Wulf Fw 190s on a very wet and muddy airstrip. Luckily for the Luftwaffe it could cope with such rough and semi-prepared airstrips. The A-5, introduced in early 1943, was an excellent fighter. Its range, speed and manoeuvrability were notably superior to the Bf 109. However, the Lavochkin La-5, favoured by Soviet fighter ace Ivan Kozhedib, was faster than both.

Chapter Eight

Ostfront Downfall

Once the German Army reached the Dnieper River in 1941 the Luftwaffe should have been overhauled in light of its vast area of operations. However, while the Soviet Union and the Western Allies sought to produce newer and better fighters and bombers, the Luftwaffe stood still. New designs were not forthcoming and German industry lagged behind requirements. Most notably, the lack of dedicated air support corps meant that the Luftwaffe's twin-engine bombers were increasingly called on to fill a tactical role rather than a strategic one.

Low-level bombing runs left them vulnerable and inappropriate close air support became their bane. The Luftwaffe's sacrifice was compounded once Hitler began to insist that his ground troops create fortresses that could withstand being surrounded. Under Hitler's mantra of 'no retreat, no surrender', it meant the Luftwaffe and the panzers had to come to the rescue every single time; in a war of attrition they could only keep this up for so long before something had to give, as in the case of Stalingrad.

General von Tippelskirch felt that Hitler's 'hedgehog', or strong point policy was the death knell of the Luftwaffe on the Eastern Front as early as the winter of 1941/42:

That winter ruined the Luftwaffe – because it had to be used for flying supplies to the garrisons of the 'hedgehogs', the forward positions that were isolated by the Russian flanking advances. The II Corps [under which he was serving] required 200 tons of supplies a day, which called for a daily average of 100 transport aircraft. But as bad weather often intervened, the actual number had to be considerably larger, so as to make full use of an interval of passable weather – on one day as many as 350 aircraft were used to reprovision this single corps. The overall strain of keeping up supplies by air to all the isolated positions on such a vast front was fatal to the future development of the Luftwaffe.

Britain and America's greatest contribution to Stalin's war effort was the strategic air campaign against Germany's cities and industries; as the battles over the Reich increased in tempo so the Luftwaffe's fighter units were siphoned off from the Eastern Front. Also, Hitler's stepping up of production of anti-aircraft artillery impacted on the production of other weapons, especially artillery. Despite this massive bomber effort during 1943, German aircraft production achieved more than 24,800 planes, of which 11,730 were fighters; it was to peak the following year with 39,800, of which a staggering 28,900 were fighters.

Nonetheless, the strategic bomber offensive made a huge contribution to the Soviets' advances because it forced the Luftwaffe to withdraw 80 per cent of its fighter squadrons and anti-aircraft batteries from the Eastern Front, and that enabled the vast Soviet victories of 1943 and, above all, 1944. The destruction of Army Group Centre would never have been possible without that withdrawal of so many Luftwaffe squadrons.

In 1943, because major offensives were no longer possible, the Luftwaffe's tactical air commands were disbanded. Instead, each air corps had to support two or three armies. It was not feasible to support the ground forces and conduct a counter-air campaign at the same time. The air forces became the servant of their allotted army group. Their role was to attack ground targets directly in front of the ground forces. This tied up about 80 per cent of the bomber force. Each month for all theatres of operation, for tactical support employing short-range bombers the Luftwaffe could put into the air about twenty units with a nominal strength of thirty aircraft each.

In particular, the air war over the German Reich precluded sending any large-scale reinforcements to bolster the Eastern Front. To make matters worse, once pilots had accumulated some combat experience over Russia they were transferred back to Germany for home defence against the bombers. The young replacements were inevitably inexperienced trainees. The Germans refused to mount standing flying patrols, instead holding their pilots poised to scramble, and as a result, interception of low-flying Soviet ground-attack aircraft was poor. Only during offensive operations could the panzers hope for continuous fighter cover.

As well as acting as flying artillery the Luftwaffe were also acting as the eyes of the German Army, as providing long-range reconnaissance for the ground forces had become a Luftwaffe mission. German aerial intelligence gathering was far from adequate. In total, the Luftwaffe's tactical reconnaissance units had available thirty Staffeln (smallest combat flying unit with a nominal strength of nine aircraft) on a monthly basis, which was not a great increase from 1941. Similarly, strategic reconnaissance units operating with the army only numbered twenty-eight Staffeln per month.

Not all was doom and gloom for the Luftwaffe on the Eastern Front: it was still more than capable of protecting the ground forces, mainly due to the superiority of its pilots and aircraft. Indeed, up until 1944 it was notable that German road and rail traffic moved in the Soviet Union largely unhindered, whereas the Red Army avoided the railways and roads during the day, except when a major offensive was being prepared. German efforts to completely destroy the Soviet rail system were partly thwarted by the Americans, who during the course of the war provided almost 2,000 locomotives and more than 11,000 rail cars. Furthermore, by 1944 Soviet tactics for defending trains had greatly improved. A crucial failure was in building up a strong, heavy bomber force, which meant many Soviet weapons factories were out of range of the twin-engine bombers and those attacks that did reach them did not disrupt production sufficiently. This left the German armed forces having to destroy Soviet armour one by one on the battlefield.

Combating Soviet tanks became a primary mission for the Luftwaffe by 1944. The German Army lacking overwhelming numbers of panzers and anti-tank guns needed the Luftwaffe, and following the failure at Kursk, all German ground-attack forces of the Stuka Gruppen, Schlachtgruppen and Schnellkampfgruppen were combined into a separate ground-attack command under General der Schlachtflieger.

Once it had become evident that the Stuka Ju-87 was too slow to survive combat conditions, units were re-equipped with the Focke-Wulf 190. The latter, designed to supplement the Messerschmitt Bf 109, soon proved itself an able ground-attack aircraft. During the second half of 1942, four fighter wings, or Gruppen, had converted to the Fw 190. Due to shortages of Fw 190 the Ju 87 units did not begin converting until the spring of 1944. Initially, II/SG 2 and I/SG 77 were the only ground-attack units equipped with Fw 190. Remarkably, by May there were seven Fw 190-equipped Schlachtgruppen on the Central and Southern sectors of the Eastern Front, totalling 197 aircraft, although most of these were in Poland and Romania.

While the growing ground-attack fleet was cause for cautious optimism, there were just thirty-one Fw 190 fighters available by June 1944, at a time when the Red Air Force stood at nearly 13,500. Production of the Fw 190 could not keep pace with demand and in early 1944, I and III Gruppen of Fighter Group 51 were forced to re-equip with the Bf 109G. The I/JG 51 returned to Bobruisk on the Central sector from Deblin-Irena in March, having completed the process.

Additionally, the loss of the Ju 87 in 1944 meant that the SD 4HI anti-tank bomb, capable of piercing 5 inches of armour, could not be delivered as regularly. This was an unwelcome degradation of capabilities, especially as the bomb also had a fragmentation effect and, carried in a container holding seventy-eight, had been used to good effect against infantry.

Once Soviet armour became increasing invulnerable to air attack new ways had to be found to destroy them. In 1943, Ju 87s and Ju 88s were fitted with a 37mm cannon and conducted operational tests in the Bryansk area. The Ju 88 did not prove to be a good platform, and whilst the Ju 87 produced good results, the Luftwaffe were unable to form large anti-tank air units. In July 1944, out of desperation Göring despatched Heinkel 177 heavy bombers to deliver low-level attacks on Soviet armour.

In June 1944, IV/JG 54 redeployed to the Eastern Front equipped with Fw 190A-8s. This Bf 109 Gruppe had retired through Romania to Germany to re-equip, but was sent to the Soviet–Polish border with sixty-four Fw 190s to cover the retreating ground troops. With JG 54 in the Baltic States and later Poland, the only Fw 190s on the main sectors of the Eastern Front were ground-attack variants numbering some 300 aircraft.

Just as Stalin's Operation Bagration was commencing, the Luftwaffe enjoyed a last-minute success. Under the designation of Operation Frantic the 8th and 15th United States Army Air Forces were operating shuttle-bombing raids against the Third Reich between the UK, Italy and the Soviet Union. This was designed to alleviate pressure on the D-Day landings in Normandy by drawing more Luftwaffe fighter units east. The Americans wanted six bases; Stalin granted them three – at Piryatin, Poltava and Mirgorod, where they were allowed to deploy more than 1,200 personnel. Frantic Joe, the very first mission, was conducted on 2 June 1944, just three weeks before Bagration commenced.

The Luftwaffe were aware of this activity and General Rudolf Meister, commanding 4th Air Corps, ordered Lieutenant Colonel Wilhelm Antrup to transfer his Heinkel III bomber wing Kampfgeschwader (KG) 55 'Greif' and Lieutenant Colonel Fritz Pockrandt's KG 53 'Legion Condor' to Minsk from the Brest-Litovsk-Random area. This brought them into range of the Frantic bases. Two other wings, KG 4 'General Wever', under Major Reinhard Grauber, and KG 27 'Boelcke', commanded by Major Rudi Kiel, were also at secret airfields near Minsk, providing a total of 367 bombers.

Hans-Detlef Herhudt von Rohden reported:

About 1000 hours on the morning of 21 June 1944, the Chief of Staff of IV Fliegerkorps in the Brest-Litovsk area received an emergency telephone call from Luftflotte 6 headquarters [under Generalfeldmarschall Robert Ritter von Greim]. Fifteen minutes later the Commanding General told his staff that a strong unit of US heavy bombers was flying to Russia. Immediately plans are made to attack. At 1500 the Commanding Officer issued the order: 'Tonight you are to attack the airfields of Poltava and Mirgorod. It is important to destroy simultaneously the US bombers.'

His report also made it clear that Meister ordered the attack on the night of the 21st, before the American bombers had even landed. The feeling was that Meister had been tipped off beforehand. The attack was scheduled for 2400 hours and the Americans were caught napping without any fighter cover. Antrup and his men were expecting a hot reception from Red Air Force Yak and Aircobra fighters, but they did not intervene.

The Luftwaffe caught seventy-three B-17 Bombers at Poltava; those German planes heading for Mirgorod inadvertently ended up there as well. Poltava was bombed and strafed for almost two hours. The Americans lost forty-seven B-17s, with nineteen others damaged but repairable, and 200,000 tons of gasoline were destroyed, halting the shuttle raids.

The American aircraft at Mirgorod were evacuated, although on the night of 22/23 June, Antrup and the others attacked Mirgorod and stayed over the target for two hours. Again, suspiciously, the Red Air Force did not contest the attack. A solitary B-17 was missed but hundreds of thousands more gallons of gasoline were destroyed.

The Red Air Force was nowhere to be seen despite the fact it was massing to support Operation Bagration, while fifty-five American Mustang fighters at Piryatin were not allowed to take off. The conclusion was that Stalin wanted the Americans out of the Soviet Union and had not lifted a finger to help. In some circles there is even speculation that he colluded in some way with the Germans. In total, the Frantic missions cost the Americans 1,030 aircraft and were widely viewed as a waste of effort and resources.

Luftwaffe personnel honour their dead; two fatalities have just been lowered into the ground whilst to the right, three have already been interred. It was clear by 1943 that the Red Air Force had wrestled air supremacy from the beleaguered Luftwaffe, which was suffering mounting casualties.

These young looking Luftwaffe aircraftsmen are both Gefreiter, or Privates First Class. The Luftwaffe had no problem recruiting well-educated and staunchly Nazi youngsters and ended up with surplus manpower.

A birdseye view from the nose of a Heinkel He 111. This bomber is flying over a frozen Russian river; all the spans of the bridge have been brought down. This may have happened in 1941–42 as the Red Army retreated, but by 1943–44, the Germans were increasingly anchoring their defensive operations on the Soviet Union's major rivers.

This Stuka and Ju 52 were photographed in March 1942. Once it became evident that the Stuka was too slow to outrun Soviet fighters, ground-attack units were re-equipped with the much more versatile Fw 190.

The initial ground-attack variant was the Fw 190F, followed by the Fw 190G-1 fighter-bomber, derived from the Fw 190A-5 but with a much greater bomb load. The Fw 190G-2 and G-3 were essentially the same but were equipped with Messerschmitt and Focke-Wulf wing racks respectively. This example carries a SC 500 bomb 500kg (1,102lb) on an ETC-5-1 rack and two 300-litre tanks under the wings for extra range.

By June 1944, there were just thirty-one Fw 190 fighters available on the Eastern Front.

Bf 109G-6s on the assembly line in Germany. The shortage of Fw 190s meant that fighter units on the Eastern Front had to continue to rely on the Bf 109. It was an excellent fighter and in the hands of an experienced pilot could outfight any Soviet fighter. However, by 1944 the Luftwaffe was stretched thin, whilst the Red Air Force was rapidly expanding.

A German He III and Ju 52 in the midst of the Russian winter. Note how the bomber's engines have been covered in an attempt to keep the frost at bay. Unable to destroy the Soviet Union's weapons factories the Luftwaffe's bomber force tried to stop equipment reaching the front by attacking Soviet railways. This, though, did not work because America kept sending replacement locomotives.

A He III being prepared for a mission. Note the externally carried bomb.

A Fw 190 operating from a concrete runway in 1942–43.

On 21 June 1944, He III from Air Wings 53 and 55 surprised American B-17 bombers at Poltava. This resulted in the destruction of forty-seven bombers and another nineteen damaged, and brought to a halt USAAF shuttle attacks on Eastern Europe.

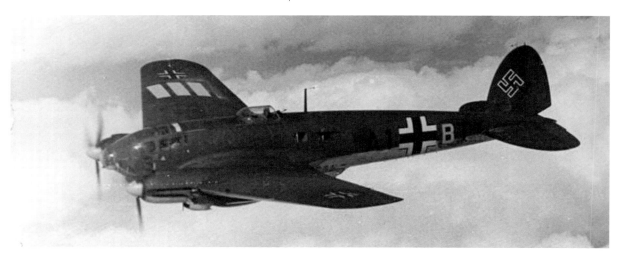

The Ju 88 proved itself to be one of the most versatile German aircraft of the war, operating in a variety of roles from fighter to low-level bomber.

Yet more sombre Luftwaffe
funerals. With its surplus
manpower taken over by the
army and its veteran pilots
redeployed to defend Germany
the young recruits sent to the
Eastern Front increasingly
became cannon fodder.

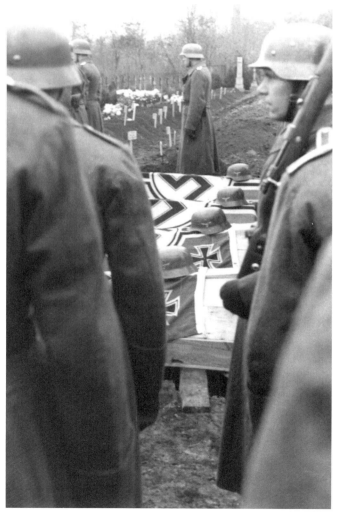

Chapter Nine

Göring's Ground War

Under Reichsmarschall Hermann Göring, despite the massive war on the Eastern Front, the Luftwaffe is best known for the Battle of Britain, the London Blitz and the desperate air battles over the Third Reich. It also played a key role in supporting Rommel in North Africa. What is not generally appreciated is that sizeable Luftwaffe units fought as ground troops in a series of key battles on the Eastern Front and in Normandy.

By the close of the winter fighting of 1941/42, German casualties on the Eastern Front had reached more than 1.6 million, not including sick, and Hitler simply did not have enough replacements. To make matters worse, the numerous components of the Wehrmacht, Heeres (army), Kriegsmarine (navy) and Luftwaffe, plus the Waffen-SS and the Reichsarbeitsdienst (RAD or Reich Labour Service), were all competing for increasingly scarce recruits.

The Luftwaffe, like the Waffen-SS, had far greater recruiting appeal for the more motivated and educated Nazi youngsters. As a result it never had problems attracting recruits to its ranks. After the Battle of Britain in 1940 the Luftwaffe found itself with more ground crew than it really needed, amounting to some 170,000 surplus personnel.

By 1941, Göring's fiefdom had expanded to almost 1,700,000 personnel, the bulk of whom were deployed in non-flying roles. The anti-aircraft branch accounted for 35 per cent (571,000) of the manpower and signal troops another 18 per cent. By late 1941, the number of men in flying units totalled 588,000, but most of these were ground support personnel or paratroops. In the summer of 1942, the German Army tried to secure them for retraining as vital infantry replacements.

Initially, when the German Army moved into the Soviet Union it was accompanied by Luftwaffe anti-aircraft or flak units. As the Red Air Force was swiftly smashed in the opening days of the invasion these were used in an anti-tank role – in particular, the Luftwaffe's 88mm flak gun supplied the best defence against the Soviet T-34 tank. By 1943, there were two Luftwaffe flak corps, amounting to eight divisions in the Soviet Union.

During the winter of 1941/42 and the Battle for Moscow, all available units were sent to bolster Army Group Centre. Because of the presence of isolated Soviet soldiers and partisans behind German lines the Luftwaffe was obliged to form emergency units to protect its airbases, depots and signal stations. In particular, the Soviet breakthrough in mid-December 1941 threatened Yukhnov – the headquarters of the Luftwaffe's 51st Fighter Group.

When General Eugen Meindl arrived at Yukhnov in January 1942, he brought with him the headquarters company of the Luftlande Sturmregiment and elements of the 7th Parachute Division. Rounding up all available units he soon put together a divisional size force for maintaining base security. This greatly bolstered the defence of Yukhnov and it was not long before Meindl was conducting offensive operations beyond the perimeter.

In early 1942, in an effort to help with manpower shortages the Luftwaffe formed seven field regiments. These rarely served together and were soon scattered across the Eastern Front. Elements of five of these regiments were involved in the relief of Demyansk. The relief of Kholm in the spring of 1942 saw the first engagement of a Luftwaffe Field Battalion, consisting of Luftwaffe volunteers from various units. As Kholm changed hands regularly the newly formed Meindl Division, later the 21st Luftwaffe Field Division, fought in this area throughout the summer and autumn.

Reichsmarschall Hermann Göring, commander-in-chief of the Luftwaffe, had it in his grasp to help the hard-pressed Army Group Centre and Army Group North on the Eastern Front, but in the name of safeguarding his own personal power base chose not to. Göring would not part with any of his forces, arguing with Hitler that transferring these 'genuinely Nationalist Socialist' young men would expose them 'to an army which still has chaplains and was led by officers steeped with the traditions of the Kaiser'. Göring got his own way and instead moved to create twenty-two Luftwaffe field divisions to support the army.

Field Marshal von Manstein was aghast at Göring hoarding troops: 'To form these excellent troops into divisions within the Luftwaffe was sheer lunacy. Where would they get the necessary close-combat training and practice in working with other formations? Where were they to get the battle experience so vital in the East? And where was the Luftwaffe to find divisional, regimental, and battalion commanders?'

General Meindl was recalled from the Eastern Front in October 1942 to organize the 13th Air Corps in Germany. Promoted to lieutenant general he was tasked with the formation of the Luftwaffe's new divisions. Former commander of the 7th Parachute Division, General Petersen was appointed as the first inspector of these units. Typically, a Luftwaffe field division on the Eastern Front had just over 6,000 men, although actual fighting strength was half that. The divisional anti-tank battalion was equipped with 50mm and 75mm guns. Its heaviest anti-aircraft weapons were 20mm and 88mm flak guns. Whilst the latter could be used in a dual anti-tank role the flak battalion only had four and its high silhouette made it vulnerable when engaging tanks. It was obvious from the start that these units were more likely to be a liability than an asset.

Göring issued Basic Order Number 3, which stated that the Luftwaffe field divisions be deployed in the Soviet Union only on defensive missions in quiet sectors. He also called on the army to welcome these units and assist with training. The divisions came under the tactical command of the army, whilst for personnel and administrative purposes they remained under Luftwaffe control.

In December 1942, the 5th Luftwaffe Field Division was deployed along the Kuban River, near the Black Sea. The 1st Division was near the city of Novgorod, north of Lake Ilmen, the 9th was sent to support Army Group North, and the 3rd and 4th divisions moved to the Vitebsk area with Army Group Centre. Reliance on the 2nd Luftwaffe Field Division resulted in the loss of Nevel on 6 October 1943 to the Red Army. Combat around the town continued into December, involving all the available Luftwaffe field divisions. The net result was that they were left in a very vulnerable position around Vitebsk and the survivors from the 2nd Luftwaffe Field Division had to be merged with the 3rd and 4th divisions.

After this indifferent, if not poor, performance the army was finally allowed to assume full control of Göring's ground forces in November 1943. About 250,000 Luftwaffe personnel joined the field divisions in 1942 and 1943; of these, 160,000 were transferred to the army. The first thing the army did was to replace nearly all the air force officers with regular army officers and reorganize them as regular army infantry divisions. The 1st and 3rd divisions were disbanded in January 1944, whilst the 5th and 15th were largely non-existent.

By early 1944, the Luftwaffe also had three flak corps: the 1st and 2nd corps were on the southern sector of the Eastern Front, while the 3rd was in France. Two new corps came into being in the second half of the year, but these were deployed to defend Germany. By 1944, in addition to the field divisions the Luftwaffe had a total of twenty-six flak divisions, again tying up valuable manpower.

By June 1944, the 4th and 6th Luftwaffe Field divisions were the only ones left in the central zone of the Eastern Front. Notably, these units under Lieutenant General Robert Pistorius and Major General Rudolf Peschel, respectively, were to play a key if brief role in defending Vitebsk in June 1944 in the face of Stalin's major summer offensive, which was designed to coincide with D-Day in Normandy.

No one believed that they were up to much, with one Luftwaffe officer admitting, 'They have the best morale. The soldiers are good, the weapons and equipment are excellent. But the training is insufficient. How can they gain experience? The division commanders were company commanders in their last assignment with the army. The majority of officers are as good as untrained in ground combat. Certainly the divisions will bravely defend their positions. But if they have to attack then it is over.'

Predictably, the 4th and 6th Luftwaffe Field divisions were lost in the maelstrom unleashed by the Red Army's Operation Bagration. The remaining Luftwaffe ground units – the 12th and 21st – were assigned to Army Group North. These four divisions, though, were but a fraction of the manpower available. Three divisions also served in the Mediterranean in Greece and Italy. Other Luftwaffe field divisions were also assigned to Army Group B in France and fought against the Western Allies. By June 1944, there were five Luftwaffe field divisions manning the Atlantic Wall; of those in France only the 16th and 17th, totalling some 20,000 men, played prominent roles in the Normandy campaign.

Göring's Luftwaffe field divisions could have been used as much needed infantry replacements to replenish Army Groups Centre and North on the Eastern Front; instead, under Luftwaffe control they added very little to the combat capabilities of the German Army, dissipated its already exhausted manpower and further muddled the chain of command. Hermann Göring's private army was a vanity project that cost the German military dearly and should never have been allowed to happen. This folly can only be attributed to Hitler's longstanding policy of divide and rule with the German armed forces. The Luftwaffe gained nothing from this whole sorry saga except the mistrust of the army at a crucial point in the war.

Two Luftwaffe Obergefreiter (leading aircraftmen) stand as honour guards over three fallen enlisted men: Otto, Walter and Helmut, killed on 11 September 1941. It is quite possible they were slain at the hands of Soviet partisans or isolated Red Army units.

Two Luftwaffe aircraftmen pay their respects to a fallen comrade, killed in 1941.

Two Flieger (aircraftmen 2nd class) and a Gefreiter (aircraftman 1st class). By the summer of 1942, Hermann Göring's Luftwaffe had about 170,000 surplus personnel, which the German Army were desperate to secure as replacement infantry. Young men such as these were destined to serve in dedicated Luftwaffe field divisions instead.

Luftwaffe 88mm flak guns on the Eastern Front, which were used in both anti-aircraft and anti-tank roles. By 1944, the Luftwaffe had two whole flak corps on the Eastern Front, tying up yet more manpower.

A German soldier examines the wreckage of what looks like the tail section of a SB-2 light bomber. It is riddled with cannon holes. Despite being the most numerous bomber of its day it suffered heavy losses in daylight attacks and was superseded by the Pe-2 and Tu-2.

The wreckage of another Soviet bomber. In the light of decreasing Luftwaffe fighter cover the German Army became increasingly reliant on anti-aircraft artillery to protect it from the Red Air Force.

More sections from shot-down Soviet aircraft that have attracted German sightseers.

The Luftwaffe moved into Russia with its own security units. In early 1942 it formed seven field regiments to help counter Soviet partisan activity; these were expanded into the Meindl Division and then a total of twenty-two Luftwaffe field divisions.

Two Luftwaffe soldiers wrapped against the cold. In the winter of 1941–42, General Eugen Meindl formed an ad hoc Luftwaffe field division to protect the headquarters of the 51st Fighter Group at Yukhnov. It proved highly successful and encouraged Göring to authorize more such formations.

This was the fate of many of the personnel drafted into the lightly equipped Luftwaffe field divisions during 1943. In the second shot the men have fled their blockhouse after being shelled or bombed. Casualties amongst the 2nd Luftwaffe Field Division were such that the survivors had to be merged with the 3rd and 4th divisions.

A Luftwaffe soldier keeps watch. In June 1944, the 4th and 6th Field Divisions found themselves defending Vitebsk right in the path of Stalin's summer offensive. The fate of Göring's field army was sealed.

Home from the front; by 1944, the Luftwaffe had little to smile about.

Chapter Ten

Red Storm Rising

By September 1943, the Eastern Front was no longer a priority for Göring's battered Luftwaffe, which was busy fending off the RAF and USAAF. German front-line strength in the East had fallen to 1,800 aircraft in early 1944 compared to 2,600 deployed in the West. Hitler's factories in 1939 produced 8,295 aircraft. Remarkably, under munitions minister Albert Speer this grew to 39,807 in 1944 but pilot attrition remained a problem.

By 1944, the turning point in the fortunes of the Red Air Force had been reached after much toil and loss of life and machines. The battles for Moscow, Stalingrad, the Kuban and Kursk witnessed its transformation from a shambles into an experienced, well organized and well run force that could match the Luftwaffe. It was now ready to assist the Red Army to push the Wehrmacht out of Mother Russia.

Bearing in mind that Hitler was now fighting in France, Italy, the Soviet Union and over Germany, the inadequate strength of the Luftwaffe fighter force was such that by mid-1944, it was incapable of covering the entire Eastern Front effectively. Growing Allied air superiority in the West and East meant that the best the Luftwaffe could achieve was temporary air superiority over combat zones. By 1944, this was no longer possible over France or Italy.

At the end of May 1944, the Luftwaffe on the Eastern Front consisted of General der Flieger Kurt Pflugbeil's 1st Air Fleet, Generaloberst Otto Dessloch's 4th Air Fleet and Field Marshal General Robert Ritter von Greim's 6th Air Fleet, which between them had a total of 2,199 aircraft, although only 1,624 were listed as available for combat. The Luftwaffe's senior authority was the 25th Regional Command, based in Minsk.

In the summer of 1944, specially trained Luftwaffe units, principally the 9th Squadron of Bomber Air Wing 3 equipped with Ju 88s and the 14th Squadron of Air Wings 27 and 55 equipped with He 111s assigned to 4th Air Corps, resumed attacking Russian railways, particularly the depots. This was in an effort to disrupt Soviet troop and supply movements. They continued these raids until the end of 1944, when fuel shortages forced their deactivation. This tactic was largely a reflection of the lack of a strategic bomber force that could have ranged further into the Soviet rear.

The Red Air Force's major effort in the summer of 1944 was Byelorussia; Operation Bagration would witness the largest tactical concentration of Soviet air power to date. The Red Air Force had 5,327 combat aircraft and another 1,007 bombers under strategic command; this comprised twenty-one fighter divisions, with 2,318 fighters, fourteen strike divisions, with 1,744 Il-2 Shturmoviks, and eight bomber divisions, with 655 medium bombers.

The 3rd, 2nd and 1st Byelorussian fronts were supported by General Khryukin's 1st Air Army, Vershinin's 4th and Rudenko's 16th. Khryukin had only just taken up his post having previously commanded the 8th Air Army during the liberation of Sevastopol and the Crimea. The latter was disbanded and its resources split between General Slyusarev in the Rava-Russkaya sector and General Krasovski in the Lvov sector. These three air armies plus elements of Papivin's 3rd Air Army on the 1st Ukrainian Front, to the north, and elements of Polynin's 6th Air Army, to the south, were able to field almost 6,000 aircraft. One third consisted of Shturmoviks – some 1,100 day and night bombers and 1,900 fighters.

Half this force was from the eleven air corps allocated to the GKO (Gosudarstvenny Komitet Oborony – State Committee for Defence) Air Reserve. Khryukin's 1st Air Army, earmarked to play a major role, was augmented with three fighter, one Shturmovik and one bomber corps, giving it a combat strength of 1,881 aircraft comprising 840 fighters, 528 Shturmoviks, 459 bombers and fifty-four reconnaissance aircraft. Similarly, Krasovski's 2nd Air Army on the 1st Ukrainian Front grew to three fighter, three Shturmovik, two bomber and one composite corps, numbering more than 3,000 aircraft ready for the breakthrough into Poland.

Zhukov took a key role in planning the air attacks on Army Group Centre, recalling:

> I also proposed that all the long-range aviation be employed in the Byelorussian action, and its operation against targets on German territory be put off until a later time. The Supreme Commander agreed, and immediately ordered Air Marshal A.A. Novikov and Air Marshal A.E. Golovanov, who was in charge of the long-range aviation, to report to me. I had worked with both these capable commanders in all major previous operations, and they had given the ground troops valuable assistance.
>
> Novikov, Golovanov, Rudenko, Vershinin and I thoroughly discussed the situation – the tasks and the operational plans of the various air armies and their cooperation with the long-range aviation, which was to strike at enemy headquarters, communication centres of operational formations, reserves

and other key targets. We also discussed the manoeuvres of the air forces of the individual fronts in the common interest. Vasilevsky was given 350 heavy long-range aircraft to support the actions of the 3rd Byelorussian Front.

On the night of 22/23 June 1944, the Red Air Force conducted about 1,000 sorties bombing German positions. More than 1,000 long-range aircraft struck German airfields at Baranovichi, Belostok, Bobruisk, Brest, Luninets, Minsk and Orsha, as well as the railways. This was nothing compared to what was to come. Unfortunately, the resulting smoke and early morning fog greatly hampered the supporting air attacks by the Red Air Force. Only Chernyakovsky's 3rd Byelorussian Front enjoyed clear weather, allowing Pe-2 bombers from the 1st Air Army to carry out 160 sorties. The ground-attack Shturmoviks had to wait until the artillery and rocket launchers had finished their work. Afterwards the Soviet infantry surged forward to seize tactical ground that would provide cover and could be exploited as a springboard for the impending breakthrough and the destruction of Hitler's Army Group Centre.

While Red Air Force numbers remained largely static at about 8,300 aircraft over the last half of 1943, from January 1944 it expanded rapidly so that by mid-year the Soviets could field just under 13,500 planes. By January 1945, this had expanded to well over 15,500. In April 1945, as the war was coming to a close, the Luftwaffe assessed the Red Air Force deployed strength as 17,000 aircraft, of which 8,000 were fighters, 4,000 Shturmoviks and 5,000 bombers. However, the overall total for the Soviet Union was 39,700.

Following the success of Operation Bagration, when the Red Army launched its attack from Warsaw towards Berlin ten air armies supported it with 15,815 aircraft. These included the latest Yak-9 and La-7 fighters and the ground-attack Shturmovik. To deceive the already hard-pressed Luftwaffe the Soviets deployed 8,818 dummy aircraft on fifty-five dummy airfields. Under General Hans-Jürgen Stumpff the Luftwaffe had 2,000 aircraft with which to shore up the disintegrating Eastern Front.

Air Chief Marshal Novikov with his subordinate air commanders massed 6,700 aircraft with the 4th, 16th and 2nd Air armies and about 800 of Golovanov's 18th Army's bombers. The real punch was provided by Sergei Rudenko's 16th Air Army, which comprised two bomber corps and four bomber divisions, two Shturmovik corps and two Shturmovik divisions, and four fighter corps and five fighter divisions, operating from 165 airfields. These were instrumental in clearing German defences, particularly on the Seelow Heights, east of Berlin. In support of the massive assault on the Nazi capital the Red Air Force flew 92,000 sorties, half of which were conducted at night.

During the final battle for Berlin, the Soviets found the Luftwaffe resisting to the last and fought 1,317 air engagements, losing 527 aircraft in the process. Novikov's reward for his role in coordinating Stalin's air armies during the battle for Berlin was to be arrested in 1946 and imprisoned for six years. He was not released until after Stalin's death, rejoining his beloved air force and commanding Soviet Long-Range Aviation during the Cold War.

There is an impression in the West that the Red Air Force did not pull its weight, and that whilst the Red Army defeated the German Army on the ground, it fell to the RAF and USAAF to defeat the Luftwaffe. This misconception is far from true. The reality is that the Red Air Force evolved and grew into a war-winning instrument of destruction. It learned how to build, repair and safeguard its aircraft. For example, in 1941 the Soviet Air Force lost one aircraft for every thirty-two sorties, and by the end of the war it was one in every 165.

Soviet long-range bombers flew 215,000 sorties, or 4 per cent of the Red Air Force's combat flights, against targets in the enemy's rear. This was not because the Soviets had little faith in bombers: on the contrary; they saw them as a weapon of great tactical value. Unlike the Western Bomber Barons, Soviet commanders were not obsessed with bombing strategic targets and bringing Nazi Germany to its knees by air power alone. Instead, they struck troop concentrations, defensive positions and ammunition depots, all of which were designed to weaken the German Army in the field.

The Red Air Force and Air Defence units flew in excess of 3 million sorties during the Second World War. Luftwaffe losses on the Eastern Front totalled 77,000 aircraft, which was 250 per cent higher than losses in all other theatres. Although the Red Air Force did not have a strategic bomber force, its medium bombers still managed to drop more than 666,000 tons of bombs. In comparison, RAF Bomber Command managed to drop 675,674 tons of bombs on Germany. Whilst the Western Allies may have starved the Luftwaffe of oil and aviation fuel it was fought and defeated by the Red Air Force in the Eastern Front air war of 1941–45.

An American airman poses with Red Air Force personnel in front of a Petlyakov Pe-2 tactical bomber, which was capable of carrying 1,600kg (3,527lb) of bombs. It was fitted with slatted dive brakes in its wings, which slowed it to a safe speed during dive-bombing attacks. German troops learned to fear this aircraft.

Another Pe-2. As part of Stalin's Operation Bagration, launched on 23 June 1943, Pe-2 bombers from 1st Air Army conducted 160 sorties in support of the 3rd Byelorussian Front.

A La-5FN getting ready for combat. Whilst Soviet pilots appreciated it as a good fighter it had its defects, not least exhaust fumes entering the cockpit. This meant that crews often flew with the canopy open. Aside from the Yak the La-5 losses were the highest of all Soviet fighters, totalling 2,591 during 1942–45.

By 1944, the Luftwaffe increasingly relied on young and inexperienced recruits to fill it ranks.

Although more than 20,000 Fw 190s were built there were never enough available on the Eastern Front. In the first shot, the two tough looking veterans' faces appear particularly fatigued.

The Bf 109 was one of the most produced fighter aircraft in history, with a total of 33,984 airframes being built from 1936 to April 1945. It was flown by three of the top scoring fighter aces, who claimed 928 victories. It was also widely flown by Germany's wartime allies, including Bulgaria, Croatia, Finland, Italy, Hungary and Romania.

A He 111 navigator charts his way to a target.

The tail end of a shot-down Soviet plane – possibly a SB-2 bomber. Throughout 1944–45 the Red Air Force pressed home its attacks with growing vigour as the German Army and the Luftwaffe began to be pushed back towards Germany.

A German souvenir hunter cuts the Red Star from the tail of a Soviet fighter. By 1944, there was no time or desire for such frivolity.

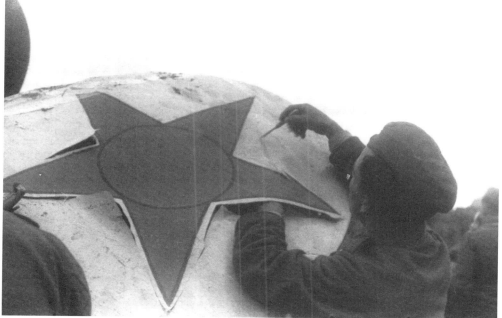

The Ju 88 bomber was used to try to stop the Red Army's advance through Byelorussia, Ukraine, Poland and then Germany itself. Such tactical ground support operations inevitably came at a cost thanks to the response of Soviet fighters.

German armourers preparing a Fw 190 for combat.

Throughout the summer of 1944, the Red Air Force harried the Wehrmacht all the way back to the very gates of Warsaw. When the Red Army launched its attack from Warsaw towards Berlin it was supported by ten air armies with 15,815 aircraft; the Luftwaffe could only oppose them with 2,000 aircraft.

Yet more Luftwaffe dead being laid to rest towards the end of the war. In total, the Luftwaffe lost 77,000 aircraft on the Eastern front, claiming 45,000 Soviet aircraft.